Reading Comprehension

Grade 7

ISBN 978-0-544-26771-8

4 5 6 7 8 9 10   0928   22 21 20 19 18 17 16

4500581664   B C D E F G

Dear Parent,

Welcome to the *Core Skills Reading Comprehension* series! You have selected a unique book that focuses on developing your child's comprehension skills, the reading and thinking processes associated with the printed word. Because this series was designed by experienced reading professionals, your child will have reading success as well as gain a firm understanding of the necessary skills outlined in national standards.

Reading should be a fun, relaxed activity for children. They should read selections that relate to or build on their own experiences. Vocabulary should be presented in a sequential and logical progression. The selections in this series build on these philosophies to insure your child's reading success. Other important features in this series that will further aid your child include:

- Interesting short reading selections appealing to adolescent readers.

- Vocabulary introduced in context and repeated often.

- Comprehension skills applied in context to make the reading more relevant.

- Multiple-choice exercises that develop skills for standardized test taking.

You may wish to have your child read the selections silently or orally, but you will find that sharing the selections and activities with your child will provide additional confidence and support to succeed. When learners experience success, learning becomes a continuous process moving them onward to higher achievements. Moreover, the more your child reads, the more proficient she or he will become.

Enjoy this special time with your child!

Sincerely,
The Educators and Staff of Houghton Mifflin Harcourt

Core Skills Reading Comprehension
GRADE 7

Table of Contents

iv

Skills Correlation

LANGUAGE ARTS SKILL	SELECTION
COMPREHENSION	
Literary Texts	
Analyzing a Poem's Structure and Meaning	8, 12
Analyzing Word Choice	2, 12
Author's Purpose	12
Author's Techniques	3, 6, 12
Cause and Effect	2, 6, 13
Characters*/Characterization	1, 2, 3, Skills Review: Selections 1–7
Comparing and Contrasting Texts in Different Genres	12
Details	2, 3
Dialogue	2, 12, Skills Review: Selections 8–14
Impact of Rhyme and Other Repetitions of Sounds	1, 12
Literary Genres	12, 14
Main Idea	1, 2, 3, 6, 13
Making Inferences	3, 6, 12
Mood and Tone	2, 13
Point of View and Narrator/Speaker	1, 2, 3, 12, 13
Sequence of Events	1, 2, 6,
Setting	1
Structure/Plot of a Literary Work	12
Summarizing Text	3, 6
Theme	6, 12
Using Text Evidence	1, 2, 13
Informational Texts	
Analyzing Interactions Between Individuals, Events, and Ideas	4, 5, 9, 14
Analyzing Word Choice and Figurative Language	6, 11
Author's Point of View	8, 9, 14
Author's Purpose	4, 5, 8, 10
Cause and Effect	7, 14
Comparing and Contrasting Writings on the Same Topic	5
Details	4, 7, 8, 9, 10, 11, 14, Skills Review: Selections 8–14
Facts and Opinions	4, Skills Review: Selections 1–7, 14
Main Idea	4, 5, 7, Skills Review: Selections 1–7, 9, 10, 14
Making Inferences	11
Relevant Information	4

Skills Correlation, continued

LANGUAGE ARTS SKILL	SELECTION
COMPREHENSION	
Informational Texts	
Sequence	4, 7
Structure of Informational Text/Organization	4, 8, 10, 14
Summarizing Text	Skills Review: Selections 1–7
Text Features	4, 5
Tone	14
Topic Sentences	Skills Review: Selections 1–7
Using Text Evidence (including to Support Claims)	5, 7, 8, 10, 11, 14, Skills Review: Selections 8–14
VOCABULARY AND DECODING	
Analogies	8, Skills Review: Selections 8–14
Antonyms	3, Skills Review: Selections 1–7
Figurative Language	3
Idioms	1
Multiple-Meaning Words	11, 13, Skills Review: Selections 8–14
Synonyms	7, 8, Skills Review: Selections 8–14
Technical Words	5, 7, 8, 9, 10
Word Meaning	1, 6, 7, 9, 11
Words in Context	3, 5, 6, 9, 14
RESEARCH AND STUDY SKILLS	
Evaluating Materials to Determine Facts	6
Evaluating Sources of Information	14
Graphic Sources	5, 6, Skills Review: Selections 1–7, 8, 9, 10, Skills Review: Selections 8–14
Hypothesizing	10
Internet Literacy	13
Outlining	8, 9
Reading for Different Purposes	3
Relevant and Irrelevant Information	9
Research Methods	2
Skimming	2
Using a Time Chart	2
Using an Encyclopedia	14

Selection 1

The Family Reunion

The Morrison family reunion is a Fourth of July tradition. These gatherings are almost always fun, but—like traditions tend to be—they aren't terribly memorable. Except for the reunion two years ago. That one was held at my aunt's house near the Llano River, and it was at that one I learned to swim.

My family arrived at my aunt's on Friday night. My cousin Jared was already there. Jared had just finished his junior year in high school. He's funny in a loud, rough kind of way, and he's mostly a real pain. In other words, he's obnoxious. Every summer he would zero in on one of us younger kids and pick on him or her the entire time. That summer two years ago, I became his target.

It started as soon as he saw me. "Hey, kid," he said, "did you ever learn to swim? Or are you going to do that doggy paddle thing again this year?"

I hung my head down, wishing that instant time travel had been invented. My obvious embarrassment in front of my other cousins didn't seem to bother Jared. He kept right on torturing me. "You know, kid, when you're in the water you remind me a lot of Aunt Tara's cocker spaniel. Pant, splash, pant, splash."

"Leave him alone, Jared," my cousin Ty said. The fact that Ty was defending me made my face turn even redder.

"Now don't get me wrong," Jared kept on. "I love your swimming style. It's a hoot. And it probably makes you popular with all your friends back home. That's how everyone swims there, right?"

I slipped away as invisibly as I could, muttering, "Jared is a blithering, bloated blowfish."

1

The next morning after breakfast, everyone under the age of twenty went down to the river. I sat around with the grownups. Despite the laughter floating up from the water, I couldn't bring myself to go there. Then the heat set in, and my "you can do it" pep talk to myself got more animated.

But it took until lunchtime before a voice in another part of my brain finally said, "Okay." I grabbed a towel, put on my flip-flops, and marched down to the river. "I may look like a cocker spaniel in the water," I thought, "but nobody cares except for blowfish."

Most of my cousins were in the river, splashing, tubing, and diving for coins. The contrast between the hot afternoon sun and the cool water was delicious. I dragged an inner tube from the bank down into the water and plopped inside it. I wasn't afraid to float down the rapids in the inner tube. That's because I stayed on the surface of the water, even when the water was moving fast.

As I approached the rapids, I saw my cousin Danny. He's a little guy and, being too small for his tube, he sat low. When the water would shoot him across the rocks, he'd bump all the way down. Each time he'd get out at the end of the rapids rubbing his backside. Danny didn't seem to mind, though. He always just ran back up the riverbank to do it again.

Not far past the rapids, the river had carved out a deep swimming hole, where a bunch of my cousins, young and old, were hanging out in their tubes. I got out of the water and watched them, wanting like crazy to be *there* instead of *here*. But, even though the surface of that swimming hole was a shimmering bluish-green, the water below was dark—and it might as well have been bottomless. Besides, Jared was there, splashing, laughing, and dunking the little kids in that menacing water. I was in agony.

As I turned to walk back to my aunt's house, my older sister Karyn swam over to the bank. She sat with me in a shallow place near some large rocks, and while we basked in the sun we talked about the river, about swimming, and about Jared.

Then Karyn did something surprising. She leaned over and whispered, "If you want to learn to swim, I'll help you."

2

My eyes narrowed. I suspected some kind of trick. But Karyn and I are tight, and all I have to do to know her real motive for something is to look in her eyes.

No doubt about it. She genuinely wanted to help. "Can you teach me right now?" I asked.

We walked over to an area that wasn't too deep. Karyn showed me how to hold my face in the water and turn it to the side to breathe. At first I balked about putting my face in, and I had to practice for a long time. But Karyn is known far and wide for her patience.

Next, my sister showed me how to move my arms in a big circle. Then we put breathing and circling together. When I could do both things at the same time, I thought I was ready. . . . Famous last thoughts.

We moved into deeper water. I could still feel the river bottom squishing between my toes. Karyn told me to float on my back. That was easy. Then she told me to turn over and float on my stomach. That was hard. All of a sudden, water rushed into my nose. I couldn't breathe, and I panicked. I started imitating a cocker spaniel again—a frightened one. So Karyn pulled my head up and helped me stand. I couldn't stop coughing and spitting out water. I told her I'd spit out a tadpole, but she shook her head and said I was imagining things. "Don't worry," she advised me calmly. "That was just your initiation dunk. It happens to everybody."

For some reason I glanced toward the bank. My mom was standing there, looking happier than I'd seen her in a long time. Her enthusiastic smile pep-talked me into trying again.

I stayed in the water with my sister-teacher so long that my fingers shriveled like old raisins. At first, I swam small circles around Karyn, staying close enough that she could grab me if necessary. Then the circles gradually got bigger. After a while, a voice in my brain, dripping with pride, said, "You're swimming. Not gracefully. But you're swimming."

When I was too tired to move anymore, Karyn and I swam to the bank. All my cousins were there, ready to high-five me, including Jared. In fact, it was Jared who helped me out of the water. Then he dramatically shook my hand and said, "Hey, little spaniel, you're not a puppy anymore." That was his idea of a compliment—one I gladly accepted.

What happened next?

How do you think Jared and the narrator's relationship changed? Write a short paragraph on another sheet of paper predicting what you think happened during the rest of the reunion.

Name _____ Date _____

A Circle the correct answer for each question.

1. What is the first clue the narrator gives the reader about Jared's personality?

    a. Jared is in high school.   c. Jared is a pain.

    b. Jared likes cocker spaniels.   d. Jared arrives early to the reunion.

2. What is the main idea of the selection?

    a. A boy learns an important lesson because of a river.

    b. A high school boy teases his younger cousin.

    c. A family reunion becomes a life-changing event.

    d. A boy learns to swim with the help of his sister.

3. Which of these statements about the narrator and his sister is evident in the selection?

    a. They care about each other.

    b. They both like to attend family reunions.

    c. They like to compete against each other.

    d. They both think Jared is a bully.

4. The narrator starts swimming like a cocker spaniel just after

    a. Karyn shows him how to move his arms in a circle.

    b. he turns over in the water and floats on his stomach.

    c. he moves into water that is deeper.

    d. Karyn and he start swimming to the bank.

B Answer the questions on the lines provided.

1. Alliteration is the repetition of the same or similar consonant sounds in words that appear close together. Read the following aloud: "Hush, hush. Sink softly into the sweet stream of sleep." All the *s* sounds have a soothing effect on the listener. What is the effect the author achieves by using alliteration in "Jared is a blithering, bloated blowfish"?

    _____

    _____

2. Compare and contrast the narrator's attitude toward doing something challenging with the attitude of his cousin Danny.

    _____

    _____

    _____

4

C Setting is the time and place in which the action of a selection takes place. In some selections, the setting is not very important, but in most cases the setting has one or more functions. Think about the setting of "The Family Reunion"; then answer, with a *yes* or *no*, whether it has each of the following functions. Explain your answers and/or give an example.

1. FUNCTION: To provide atmosphere (the mood or feeling of the selection) or to contribute to the selection's emotional effect

   _____

   _____

   _____

2. FUNCTION: To help reveal what a character is like

   _____

   _____

   _____

3. FUNCTION: To act as the antagonist (the character or force that the main character has to struggle against)

   _____

   _____

   _____

4. FUNCTION: To move the action of the plot forward

   _____

   _____

   _____

   Which function of the setting do you think is *most* important in "The Family Reunion"?

   _____

D Write the correct word next to each meaning. If you have trouble choosing an answer, look back
to the selection to see how the word is used.

reunion	dunking	imitating
initiation	obnoxious	enthusiastic
blithering	basked	balked
rapids	panicked	shriveled
agony	squishing	embarrassment
genuinely	animated	memorable

1. unpleasant to be around _____

2. talking foolishly _____

3. felt fear or anxiety _____

4. a meeting or gathering _____

5. stubbornly refused _____

6. dried up _____

7. acting, pretending to be like _____

8. an introduction to something new _____

9. truly, actually _____

10. pushing under _____

11. excited and encouraging _____

12. warmed oneself _____

13. an uneasy or self-conscious feeling _____

14. squirting or oozing _____

15. great pain _____

16. worth remembering _____

17. fast-moving water _____

18. lively _____

E An idiom is an expression that means something different from the literal meaning of each word it is composed of. An example of an idiom is "It's raining cats and dogs." On the lines below, write what you think is the meaning of each underlined idiom. Look for clues to the meaning in the sentence or short paragraph. You can also look up the key word in a dictionary.

1. A lot of people don't like to be around Jared. He's funny—but in a loud, rough kind of way. Actually, he's <u>a real pain</u>.

_____

_____

2. Every summer Jared would <u>zero in on</u> one of the younger kids and pick on him or her the entire weekend.

_____

_____

3. Jared told the narrator that his swimming style was a <u>hoot</u> and that it probably made him popular with his friends.

_____

_____

4. Principal Jones gave a speech to the whole class about helping to keep the school clean. He talked about our taking pride in the environment. Finally, he asked us to <u>give him a hand with</u> his latest school clean-up project.

_____

_____

5. Karim didn't seem to get along very well at school at first. His grandmother said he was <u>a square peg in a round hole</u>. That made Karim mad, so he joined the band and made some good friends.

_____

_____

6. The hikers had walked all day and then set up their camp. When they finally settled down in their sleeping bags that night, they <u>slept like rocks</u>.

_____

_____

Selection 2

A Surprise for Cole

Cole's dad was unusually late picking him up on Friday night. Cole didn't say anything to his mother, but he was a little worried. His dad was almost always on time. Cole sat quietly, tracing the stitching on his overnight bag.

Finally, the phone rang. Cole jumped up. His mom rushed to the kitchen to answer it. "He's on his way," she announced with relief. "He got tied up at the office."

Soon Cole and his dad were in the car driving to his dad's apartment. An odd smile kept pushing up the corners of his dad's mouth. It irritated Cole just a little, considering how worried he'd been until about ten minutes ago. "Sorry about that," his dad said. "Something came up at the office. I know it's too late to do much tonight. But," he added, "I have a special day planned tomorrow. I hope you don't mind."

"No problem," Cole said. He silently forgave his dad for the weird smiling. Deep down, he knew their weekends together were as important to his dad as they were to him.

The next morning, golden rays spilled through Cole's bedroom window. Saturday had come. By the time his dad got up, Cole was already dressed and eating breakfast. His dad said, "You're in a hurry this morning. Let me finish this cup of coffee, and we'll be on our way. Okay?"

The highway was a gray stripe through green countryside. On either side, wildflowers bounced in the wind. Their red and yellow heads moved up and down like fishing bobs on a lake. Cole's dad slowed the car and turned right onto a farm road. Then he turned again, this time onto a dirt road that sliced the pasture.

Cole's dad stopped the car. "Well, what do you think?"

Cole looked to the left, then to the right. "What do you mean?" he asked.

His dad laughed softly. "This is our farm. This is why I was late last night. I had to sign the papers." Cole's eyes widened and his mouth fell open, but he couldn't speak a word.

Selection 2
Core Skills Reading Comprehension, Grade 7

Cole and his dad walked through the pasture to a row of graceful trees. The deep green live oaks and giant cottonwoods bowed over a narrow creek. The creek babbled like a child. The sun's rays sparkled on the water. Cole and his dad sat on the bank. "What do you think?" his dad said quietly, sounding slightly afraid of his son's answer.

Cole forced his eyes away from the creek and faced his dad. "I love it," he almost whispered.

Cole's dad, grinning, led him toward the old farmhouse beyond the creek. "I thought we could come here on the weekends," his dad said. "We could fix up the house together. I could use the help. Wait until you see it. It's been empty for more than forty years."

"Who used to live here?" Cole asked.

"I don't know," his dad replied. "The agent said the last owner never used the house. He just let it go to ruin. He's the person who sold the farm." They reached the farmhouse, and for the second time in one day, Cole didn't know what to say. This was the tallest, oldest, most run-down house he'd ever seen. He loved it.

"Wow!" Cole yelled. "Cool house! This is great!" Cole started running. His dad yelled, "Cole, slow down. You can't trust those steps." But Cole couldn't hear the last warning. It came just as his leg went through a rotten board. The bottom half of his body disappeared, swallowed by the steps.

Cole's dad raced toward him. "Are you okay, Cole? Can you move?" he asked. Panic distorted his voice.

Cole groaned a little as his dad pulled him up from the step. "I think I'm all right. Nothing's broken." While his dad checked his legs, Cole lay on the porch. His head turned toward the jagged hole. "Dad, I think there's something down there. Go look." Cole's dad ignored him as he continued to check for broken bones.

9

"Dad, we need to investigate," Cole said. By now, he'd forgotten about his legs.

Finally, his dad looked inside the hole. "Okay. But you stay here. I'll go in this time." He squeezed through the hole, landing with a thud. When he came back up, he was holding a metal box caked in decades of dirt. He and Cole used a pocketknife to remove the dirt and pick the small, rusting lock that kept the box sealed.

"Wow!" Cole and his dad said at the same time. A small leather box and a dirty envelope were inside. Nestled in the box was a World War II Medal of Honor. Even now, the eagle shined and the ribbon looked fresh. The envelope contained a certificate and a small, framed photograph. "Horace Mickel," Cole's dad said, reading the name on the certificate. "I'd say this medal and this house belonged to him."

"Who was Horace Mickel, Dad? Do you think he left anything else under those steps?" Cole asked. "Or in the house?" he added eagerly.

"Could be," Cole's dad replied. "Let's forget the steps for now. If you think you can get yourself up, we'll start looking for the answers to your questions inside."

Cole's dad unlocked the front door. He held Cole's elbow as Cole hobbled inside. A breeze came in with them, disturbing dust that had sat comfortably for forty years. Spiderwebs as fine as lace capped their heads. "This is great, Dad. It looks like Mr. Mickel left everything behind. There are bound to be clues everywhere."

10

"I think you're right, Cole. But I have an idea. Let's not try to find all of our answers today. Let's make this last a while. Let's make this our weekend project, and we'll come to know Mr. Mickel a little at a time, just like friends normally do. Is it a deal?" He stuck out his hand."

"Deal," said Cole, shaking hands. "I think I'll put this photograph above the fireplace. Then we'll know where to find Mr. Mickel when we come back."

How will their relationship change?

Use clues that you picked up while reading the selection to write a short paragraph on another sheet of paper. Describe how the relationship between Cole and his dad will change as they fix up the farmhouse.

11

A **Circle the correct answer for each question.**

1. Why is Cole's dad late to pick him up?

   a. He had to go to a meeting.

   b. He had to sign papers.

   c. He forgot that it was Friday.

   d. He had to go see the farm.

2. What is Cole's surprise?

   a. the early breakfast

   b. the drive through the country

   c. the metal box

   d. the farm

3. Cole's dad is afraid that

   a. Cole will not like the farm.

   b. he and Cole will not be able to fix up the farmhouse.

   c. Cole cannot find out who Horace Mickel is.

   d. he cannot afford to buy the farm.

4. Which of these details does *not* provide evidence about how Cole and his mom were feeling in the first two paragraphs?

   a. Cole traces the stitching on his overnight bag.

   b. Cole jumps up when the phone rings.

   c. Cole's mom rushes to the kitchen to answer the phone.

   d. Cole's mom announces with relief that Cole's dad is on the phone.

5. In the seventh paragraph, how does Cole probably feel?

   a. astonished   **b.** unhappy   **c.** puzzled   **d.** angry

B **Answer the questions on the lines provided.**

1. Read the third and fourth paragraphs. Describe how Cole's and his dad's points of view are different in this part of the selection.

   _____

   _____

   _____

2. Read the tenth paragraph. What is the mood of the selection at this point? What language does the author use to create this mood?

   _____

   _____

   _____

3. Read the dialogue in the last four paragraphs of the selection. What does this dialogue accomplish?

_____

_____

_____

C Details in a selection tell *where, when, why, how, who,* and *what* about the topic and/or the action. Skim the selection to find these details or facts. Write the key words that help you locate the information, and then answer the questions. One is done for you.

1. Where did Cole's dad take his son after he picked him up Friday night?

   picked him up—to his apartment _____

2. What kinds of trees were on the farm?

   _____

3. How many years had the farmhouse been empty?

   _____

4. Who told Cole's dad about the former owner?

   _____

5. What did Cole and his dad use to open the box?

   _____

6. What is Cole's overnight bag a clue to?

   _____

   _____

   _____

D **Read the selection.**

The Congressional Medal of Honor

In 1863, President Abraham Lincoln first awarded the Congressional Medal of Honor. It was created to encourage the Union soldiers in the Civil War and "increase efficiency in the navy." Many decades have passed since then, and the medal has grown into a special symbol of bravery and sacrifice. Today, the Medal of Honor is the highest U.S. military decoration given.

In 1918, Congress defined what is expected of a Medal of Honor winner. Congress said that the person had to be a member of the military. Congress also said the person must be engaged in conflict with an enemy of the United States. And, finally, and most importantly, the person should show bravery and risk to his or her life "above and beyond the call of duty."

Of the millions of United States citizens who have gone into battle, only a little over 3,000 have been given the Medal of Honor. Most of the people who have received this medal did not survive the battle for which they were honored. A few did, however. All of these medal holders, living or dead, have shown their bravery by going into heavy fire or going behind enemy lines. Some have even given their lives to save their fellow soldiers.

By 1963, the requirements for a member of the Navy, the Army, and the Air Force to receive the Medal of Honor were made the same. Today, only the designs of the medals differ from one branch of the service to the other. All three feature an inverted, gold star. They hang from blue ribbons that can be worn around the neck. Each ribbon ends in a "knot" that is embroidered with thirteen stars. These stars represent the thirteen original American colonies. The Air Force and Army medals hang from a bar that reads "valor." The Navy medal hangs from an anchor. Personnel of the Marine Corps and Coast Guard receive the Navy version of the medal.

The Medal of Honor has changed from being a simple reward and has grown into something much more valued and respected. It is only for those who have risked their lives in an outstanding way for the sake of others. During World War II, the Korean War, and the Vietnam War, more Medals of Honor were given to the dead than to the living. Because of this, the medal has acquired a special, serious quality. The living Medal of Honor holders know that they are lucky. They rarely speak of glory; they mainly speak of their gratitude. They do not say they "won" the medal. They prefer to say that they and their fellow soldiers "earned" it.

14

Each paragraph about the Medal of Honor has two or more details that support a main idea. Read the following ideas from the five paragraphs in the selection. Label each *Main Idea* or *Detail*.

Paragraph 1

_____ **a.** The medal was created to encourage Union soldiers.

_____ **b.** The medal is the highest military decoration awarded.

_____ **c.** President Lincoln first awarded the Medal of Honor.

Paragraph 2

_____ **a.** The person must be a member of the military.

_____ **b.** The person must be engaged in conflict with an enemy.

_____ **c.** Bravery "above and beyond" must be shown by the person.

_____ **d.** Congress defined what is expected of someone who is awarded the Medal of Honor.

Paragraph 3

_____ **a.** All medal holders have shown their bravery.

_____ **b.** Only a little over 3,000 Medals of Honor have been given.

_____ **c.** Most soldiers did not survive the battle.

_____ **d.** A few soldiers did survive.

Paragraph 4

_____ **a.** All three medals have an inverted, gold star.

_____ **b.** Only the designs of the medals differ from one branch to another.

_____ **c.** The Navy medal hangs from an anchor.

Paragraph 5

_____ **a.** Medal holders prefer to say they "earned" their medal.

_____ **b.** The medal has a special, serious quality.

_____ **c.** A person awarded the medal rarely speaks of glory.

_____ **d.** Medal holders speak of gratitude.

Cole found a box containing a Medal of Honor that had probably belonged to Horace Mickel. Who was this man, and what happened to him? Think about the clues given in the selection that Cole could pursue.

1. If Cole wants to find out more about Horace Mickel, what research tools would you suggest he use?

_____

_____

_____

2. What do you think he should do first in his search for the identity of Mr. Mickel?

_____

_____

_____

3. What should he do second?

_____

_____

_____

4. What should he do third?

_____

_____

_____

Selection 2
Core Skills Reading Comprehension, Grade 7

F Do you think Cole will find out who Horace Mickel is? Who do you think he will turn out to be? Is Horace still alive? How old would he be?

Consider writing a story about Cole's search for Horace Mickel. Think about a main idea for your story. Use the boxes below to help you organize your ideas and the order of what will happen in your story.

What is the main idea of your story?

What happens first?

What happens next?

How does your story end?

Most autobiographies and biographies are arranged in a logical order by date. Dates are important in doing research. They can help you skim a selection and create an outline of information quickly. You can scan for important happenings by noticing the dates in a selection. Read this short biography of a Medal of Honor holder and fill out the time chart below.

The Medal of Honor of all branches of the armed services displays a woman's face. The Army's, Navy's, Marine Corps's, and Coast Guard's medals have the Greek goddess Athena. The medal for the Air Force features the face of the Statue of Liberty. Despite these facts, Dr. Mary Walker is the only woman ever awarded a Medal of Honor.

Mary Walker became a doctor in 1855. After the Battle of Bull Run in 1861, she helped take care of the 1,100 wounded. In 1863, she served close to the battlefield. She often went deep into enemy territory to deliver needed medical supplies.

Dr. Walker may have also performed an even more dangerous service. It is believed that she acted as a spy for Union troops against the Confederacy. She often rode behind enemy lines to discover and carry important information about enemy troop movements. In 1864, Dr. Walker was captured by the Confederate Army and held as a prisoner. She was released later that year in a prisoner exchange.

The Medal of Honor was given in 1865 to those who had shown "soldier-like qualities" in the Civil War. Dr. Mary Edwards Walker had certainly shown such qualities. President Andrew Johnson awarded her the medal.

In 1866, Dr. Walker began to speak out for women's right to vote. This was called the suffragette movement. She died in 1919, just months before the Nineteenth Amendment was passed. This amendment gave women the right to vote.

Time Chart	
Date	**Event**
1853	Mary Walker enrolls in medical school.
1855	

Selection 3

The Unwritten Laws

Sometimes it's hard being an older sibling, especially when you have a brother like mine. Chris is so cheerful all the time. Plus, he's excited about starting middle school next year. It's only February, and he's still in fifth grade, but he's already excited. I've told him again and again that there's not so much to be excited about, but so far I haven't convinced him. Take lockers, for instance. You see, of all the reasons there are to go to middle school, my brother thinks having a locker is the best reason of all.

I've tried to explain to Chris that there are some middle-school laws that aren't written in any school handbook. They're not posted in the hallway or on the bulletin board in the office. They just exist. Only middle-school students know what they are. They're a secret to everyone else. I started off with the laws about lockers.

First, I told him he'd better start practicing deep-knee bends. I described the lockers at our school. Two rows of lockers line every hallway. One of the laws every middle-school kid knows is that the tall kids get the lockers on the bottom. If you're tall—and my brother is—then you ought to practice deep-knee bends every morning before you get to school. That will be the only thing that keeps you in shape. Plus, you'll have to learn how to bend with one arm up in the air. I explained that you use

the arm to protect your head. That's because the rule that makes tall kids get the bottom lockers is the same rule that gives short kids the top lockers. While you're on your knees, I told him, they're on their toes. At least once a day, the kid on top loses his or her balance. The kid's books fall with the kid, and *there*—I say with a short demonstration—is where your arm comes in handy.

He watched carefully and seemed to understand. I thought I'd convinced him that his first locker wasn't going to be the highlight of middle school, but I was wrong. He smiled and started doing deep-knee bends. He's really industrious. He's also amazing.

So I tried to give him another lesson in locker reality. We talked about the locks. I explained that a lock never works when you're in a hurry. It will work any other time, but not if you're in a rush. That means if you don't remember to get your track shoes out before you slam the door shut, you're going to be late for gym. The coach isn't going to listen to any excuses, and you and all the other kids who couldn't get their lockers open will run extra laps. You can blame the second law of lockers. Every middle-school kid knows that a lock has only one good spin a day. After that, you have to beg, scream, and fight to get it open. You also have to be ready to take the consequences when you're late for class.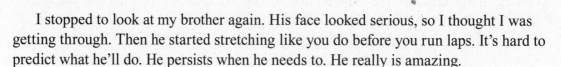

I stopped to look at my brother again. His face looked serious, so I thought I was getting through. Then he started stretching like you do before you run laps. It's hard to predict what he'll do. He persists when he needs to. He really is amazing.

Well, since laws one and two didn't seem to make much difference, I moved on to the third law. That's the law of egg-salad sandwiches. This law, I explained, says that if even one kid in the whole school brings an egg-salad sandwich for lunch, that kid has the locker above yours. Your nose finds your locker before you do. The smell attaches itself like an evil glue to everything in your locker, including your gym clothes. People won't make fun of you, of course. They know you didn't get to choose your locker. However, you can't expect them to eat lunch with you.

I looked closely at my brother. His eyebrows met in the middle. He seemed to be struggling to understand all these lessons and laws. Then he ran into the bathroom. He came out holding a can of air freshener. "This should take care of law number three," he said. I shook my head. I had serious doubts about winning this battle.

I had only one locker law left—the surprise clean-out. I explained that at least once in every grading period, your homeroom teacher makes the whole class clean out their lockers. You never know when these days are coming, and if you aren't prepared, the word *embarrassed* is not enough to describe how you feel. Middle-school teachers know just the right time for a clean-out. It's always the day that you've forgotten to take home your dirty gym shorts. It's the day your overdue library books are bursting to get out. It's the day a colony of fruit flies has escaped from the science lab and finds the rotting apple in your locker. It's the day the Valentine card you got for the girl who sits next to you in homeroom falls out and lands at the girl's feet.

I thought for sure that mentioning the Valentine card would do the trick. Chris gets bashful around girls. I waited for him to say something. He disappeared again, this time into his bedroom. When he came out, he handed me a card. I opened it and read it out loud, "To my sister on Valentine's Day." My brother smiled and gave me a hug. It was a little embarrassing—but what an amazing kid! He's going to love middle school. And he might find it exciting after all.

Ⓐ Circle the correct answer for each question.

1. Which of these is ***not*** an unwritten law that the narrator explains to Chris?

    a. A lock never opens when you are in a hurry.

    b. Tall students are assigned the lockers on the bottom row.

    c. You must keep you locker spotlessly clean at all times.

    d. If a smelly sandwich is brought to school, it will be in the locker above yours.

2. According to the narrator, how does Chris act around girls?

    a. bossy

    b. talkative

    c. comfortable

    d. bashful

3. What is the main idea of the ninth paragraph?

    a. A homeroom teacher will announce a locker clean-out when there is something embarrassing inside the locker.

    b. Dropping a Valentine card during a locker clean-out can be embarrassing.

    c. Dirty gym shorts and overdue library books are often inside lockers when a teacher announces a locker clean-out.

    d. Students must be prepared for Valentine cards, dirty gym shorts, and library books to fall out of their locker.

4. Why does the narrator keep calling her brother "amazing"?

    a. He gives her a Valentine's card and a hug.

    b. He is cheerful and excited about middle school.

    c. He seems to understand what she says about lockers.

    d. He is not bothered by the idea of egg-salad sandwiches in lockers.

5. Based on the selection, which of these ideas would Chris *most likely* believe is true?

    a. You can always learn from people older than you.

    b. The future is more interesting than the past.

    c. Every problem has a solution.

    d. There is no way to avoid challenges.

6. Which of these excerpts from the selection contains a simile?

    a. *While you're on your knees, I told him, they're on their toes.*

    b. *The smell attaches itself like an evil glue to everything in your locker, including your gym clothes.*

    c. *His eyebrows met in the middle. He seemed to be struggling to understand all these lessons and laws.*

    d. *It's the day your overdue library books are bursting to get out.*

7. Which of these does the author use in the narrator's explanations about the lockers?

    a. rhymes

    b. statistics

    c. stories about teachers and principals

    d. exaggerations

B **Answer the questions on the lines provided.**

1. Does the narrator, Chris, or both of the characters change their way of thinking during the course of the selection? Explain your answer.

_____

_____

_____

2. Write a brief summary of the selection.

_____

_____

_____

22

C A reader can gain clues about a character from what he or she says, thinks, and does—as well as from things that other characters think and say about him or her. The chart below provides clues about Chris.

is cheerful all the time	is thoughtful	is industrious
persists when he needs to	is excited about going to middle school	practices what his sister says he will have to do as a result of having a locker

1. Based on these clues, write a short paragraph about the type of person Chris is.

   _____

   _____

   _____

   _____

   _____

2. Now use what you have in item 1 to write a short paragraph describing Chris's first day in the middle school.

   _____

   _____

   _____

   _____

   _____

   _____

D On each line are two words that are antonyms, or words that are opposite in meaning. Circle the antonyms.

1. cheerful	abrupt	depressed	talkative
2. reject	explain	accept	justify
3. intelligent	upset	serious	humorous
4. scatter	forget	late	gather
5. tightening	swinging	stretching	teaching
6. happy	amazing	spotless	ordinary
7. practice	protect	attack	demonstrate
8. unashamed	embarrassed	snared	dirtied
9. departed	started	showed	arrived
10. rested	struggled	pressured	convinced

E Choose a word from below to complete each sentence.

siblings	consequences	highlight
bashful	reality	industrious
attach	persist	balance

1. To be really shy is to be _____

2. To stick to, or cling to, something is to _____.

3. Brothers and sisters are called _____

4. To continue doing something even when it is hard is to _____

5. The best part of an experience is the _____

6. To be busy and hardworking is to be _____

7. What really happens or exists is called _____

8. When an object's weight is placed equally, it is in _____

9. The effects of something that happened earlier are the _____

Name _____ Date _____

 The narrator in "The Unwritten Laws" tries to pass along to her brother ideas on how to survive in middle school. Most schools have a handbook that lets students know the rules for their school. Read this section from a school handbook and answer the questions.

Library Information

Mrs. Mitchell, the school librarian, would like all students to know that they are expected to adopt a quiet manner when using the library. Students are studying and reading and need a good atmosphere to work in.

General student hours are:
Monday–Wednesday 9 a.m.–4 p.m.
Thursday and Friday 8 a.m.–3:30 p.m.

Bus students only:
Monday–Friday 7 a.m.–8 a.m.

On Tuesday afternoons at 3:00, a "homework help" math study group meets in the library's Sierra Room. A student must have a pass from the principal and a note from parents or guardians. If you would like to join, put your name on a sign-up sheet in Mrs. Mitchell's office.

Have a written list of math questions and problems ready to show Mrs. Mitchell.

1. How late is the library open on Tuesdays? _____

2. Who is the library open to from 7 a.m. to 8 a.m.? _____

3. What 3 pieces of paper must you have in order to participate in homework help?

   _____

   _____

4. What piece of paper should you sign? _____

5. What list do you need to prepare for Mrs. Mitchell?

   _____

   _____

6. When does the library open on Thursdays to all students? _____

7. Where does the homework help group meet? _____

8. Why are students expected to be quiet in the library?

   _____

   _____

Selection 4: Paired

The Wright Brothers

When the Wright brothers were little boys, their father brought home a strange toy. The boys probably thought it resembled some type of bird-bat hybrid. The toy was made of paper and wood, and a twisted rubber band supplied the power. When the two boys, Wilbur and Orville, tossed it into the air, it would fly across the room. Later, when the toy broke, they experimented and made their own flying toys. From then on, the Wright brothers were interested and excited by anything that could fly. In that year of 1878, their interest was quite unusual since planes had yet to exist. Even cars had not been invented yet. People traveled by train, horse and buggy, and bicycle.

In 1893, the two young men started a bicycle shop. By that time, the first cars, called motorcars, had just started being seen around town. The motorcars made so much irritating noise that they probably should have been banned. However, the brothers were more interested in planes and flying than in motorcars. They had read about a man named Otto Lilienthal, who had built a plane that did not have an engine. He called it a glider. Unfortunately, Lilienthal and his glider crashed.

Lilienthal's doomed experiment in no way discouraged Orville and Wilbur. They began to read everything they could about flying. More than likely, they read day and night to absorb so much new information. They also wrote to the Smithsonian Institution to ask for help. A man at the museum sent them all the latest books and articles about flying.

Orville and Wilbur had read that balance and control were key to flying a glider. But how could an airplane be kept in balance? How could a pilot control the plane, making it go up and down or left and right? They probably felt overwhelmed by such questions.

The Wright brothers decided that the wings of the plane should be flexible and movable at the ends. One wing could be curved up by a control, while the other was curved down. In this way, the wings would meet the air at different angles, and one would get greater lift from the air than the other. This would make it possible to steer and balance the plane. They also decided that they needed something called a rudder. Similar to what was on a boat, the rudder would be a flat piece on the back of the plane. By moving it from side to side, the glider could be steered by a pilot.

The two brothers went to work and built a model of their idea. They flew the small glider like a kite. From the ground below, they were able to work its controls by pulling on ropes attached to its wings and rudder. The experiment was a success, and their model flew. No doubt they were tremendously happy that day.

By 1900, they had finished work on their life-size glider. They chose Kitty Hawk in North Carolina for the flight test. At first, their glider went only a few feet. As they experimented and adjusted the controls, the flights kept getting longer.

Then, in 1903, they built a plane with an engine. Again, they went to the soft sands of Kitty Hawk to test it. They wanted to be the first men to fly a powered airplane. Early on the morning of December 17, 1903, the two brothers were ready. They both had worked so long and so closely together on their dream that they tossed a coin to see who would try to fly the plane first. Orville won the toss.

It was very windy, and Orville had a difficult time controlling the airplane. However, even though the flying machine went only 100 feet and stayed in the air 12 seconds, it was enough. Orville had made the first powered flight in history. Wilbur went up in the plane next and managed to stay in the air almost a minute!

The two brothers, overjoyed with what they had done together, sent a telegram. It was to the person who had ignited their passion for flying so long ago. They wired their father the following: "Success. Four flights. Inform press. Home Christmas."

Name _____ Date _____

Circle the correct answer for each question.

1. Paragraphs 1 and 2 are *mainly* about the Wright brothers' interest in

    a. flying toys

    b. human flight

    c. bicycles

    d. motorcars

2. The Wright brothers started researching the concept of flying machines soon after they

    a. read about the unsuccessful flight of a glider

    b. understood which parts a plane would need to operate

    c. were given a toy that could fly across a room

    d. made their first flying toy

3. In paragraphs 1 and 2, which information is *least* relevant to the main topic of the selection?

    a. Orville and Wilbur's father gave them a toy that could be tossed into the air.

    b. Orville and Wilbur made their own flying toys.

    c. In 1893, only a few motorcars could be seen around town.

    d. A man named Otto Lilienthal had built a glider.

4. If the author had divided the selection into sections and given each section a heading, what would be the *best* heading for paragraphs 3–5?

    a. Discovery

    b. Wings and Rudders

    c. Researching and Planning

    d. Learning How to Control a Plane

5. Which of these questions *cannot* be answered using information from paragraphs 8–10?

    a. Why was Wilbur able to stay up in the air longer than Orville?

    b. What was the goal of Wilbur and Orville Wright?

    c. What were the weather conditions on the day of the Wright brothers' first flight?

    d. Why did Orville get to fly the plane first?

6. Which of these *best* describes the general organization of the selection?

    a. The problem encountered by the Wright brothers is presented, followed by the potential solutions they tried.

    b. Events related to the first flight of a powered airplane are described in the order in which they occurred.

    c. The two brothers who first flew a powered airplane are compared and contrasted.

    d. The various effects caused by the Wright brothers' flight achievements are described.

B **Answer the questions on the lines provided.**

1. What is the *most likely* reason that the author includes questions in paragraph 4?

   _____

   _____

2. Explain how the Wright brothers' father and Otto Lilienthal were factors in the brothers' eventual achievements.

   _____

   _____

C **When you research a subject, you usually can find many facts about it. Statements of fact are empirically true—that is, they are based on observation, experience, or both—and can be supported by evidence. However, sometimes you may find information that is someone's opinion. A statement of opinion is a belief; it is usually based on the person's emotions or understanding of something. It is important to be able to tell the difference between a statement of fact and a statement of opinion. Write an *F* by each statement of fact from the selection and an *O* by each statement of opinion.**

_____ 1. The boys probably thought it resembled some type of bird-bat hybrid.

_____ 2. Later, when the toy broke, they experimented and made their own flying toys.

_____ 3. The motorcars made so much irritating noise that they probably should have been banned.

_____ 4. They began to read everything they could about flying.

_____ 5. More than likely, they read day and night to absorb so much new information.

_____ 6. Orville and Wilbur had read that balance and control were key to flying a glider.

_____ 7. They probably felt overwhelmed by such questions.

_____ 8. The Wright brothers decided that the wings of the plane should be flexible and movable at the ends.

_____ 9. The experiment was a success, and their model flew.

_____ 10. No doubt they were tremendously happy that day.

_____ 11. They wanted to be the first men to fly a powered airplane.

Selection 5: Paired

Soaring High

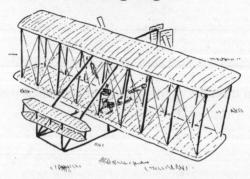

For thousands of years, humankind has dreamed of flying like the birds. With the fulfillment of this age-old dream, Wilbur and Orville Wright gave the world the freedom to soar above the clouds. In addition, their fascination with human flight resulted in experiments and inventions that would change the world forever.

Their Childhood

Wilbur and Orville were two of seven children born to Bishop Milton Wright and Susan Catharine Wright. Their father's work forced them to move frequently. Even so, they lived in an environment in which children were encouraged to follow their interests. Their parents taught them strong values and supported them when problems came their way.

When they were young boys, their father gave them a flying toy made from paper and bamboo, powered by a rubber band motor. The experience of watching this small toy soar across their house inspired them. Wilbur wanted to build a flying machine large enough to carry the boys into the air. The brothers tried to learn all they could about the science of flight.

Orville was extremely curious about mechanical things as a child. He was always building and repairing things. When he was only a teenager, he began a printing business, which his brother later joined.

Early Accomplishments

In 1893, the two brothers established a bicycle business in Dayton, Ohio. What began as a rental and repair shop soon became a sales shop, carrying more than a dozen brands. Yet the fierce competition in the bicycle business was discouraging. Besides that, the brothers needed more challenges.

Wilbur had never forgotten his childhood dream of building a full-sized flying machine. The brothers began to study the work of aircraft designers from the past. For example, Leonardo da Vinci was a famous Italian inventor and artist from the late 1400s. He filled notebooks with designs for fantastic flying machines. What was new about the Wright brothers' design approach was that they began experimenting.

A workroom behind the bike shop became their laboratory. They built kites and model gliders to help turn Wilbur's dream into a reality.

The Wright brothers had set out to solve a problem that had challenged better-known aviation pioneers for centuries. Wilbur and Orville worked alone and with little training. Although they were talented, much of their success resulted from their background and their early experiences with mechanics.

Achieving Their Goal

The Wright brothers had read accounts of the discoveries made by earlier scientists. However, they found that the earlier data were unreliable, and they wanted data they could trust. As a result, they decided to build a wind tunnel to carry out their own tests and achieve their goal. Air would be forced through the wind tunnel with great power. Using this device, they could test the effects of wind and air pressure on different designs. Their experience with the bike shop had taught them that machines should be controllable.

These tests led the Wright brothers to accomplish a great deal in the field of flight.
- They were the first people to understand the value of a long, thin, curved wing shape to provide lift.
- They created a pulley system that bent the wings' shape in flight. This made the wings stable and easier to control.
- They used their research into wing shapes to design the first working airplane propellers.
- They mounted movable surfaces called elevators in front of the wings. These adjustable, flat pieces were used to raise and lower the plane.
- They added a pair of rudders in back to control the plane's side-to-side motion.

When the Wright brothers could not find an engine manufacturer, they designed their own engine. This lightweight, 12-horsepower engine powered the glider. Orville made the first successful flight test in Kitty Hawk, North Carolina, in 1903. The flying machine remained aloft for 12 seconds. The brothers celebrated their success.

Affecting the Future

The Wright brothers are probably best known for their invention of a flying machine. However, they also made another important contribution through their approach to the technology of flight. Aviators today still use the Wright brothers' experimental methods. Many engineers still test their own aircraft and improve their designs based on the results.

A **Circle the correct answer for each question.**

1. Which part of the Wright brothers' first plane served to make the plane move from side to side?

    a. rudder

    c. pulley system

    b. elevators

    d. propellers

2. What is the *most likely* reason that the author includes the story of the flying toy in the section "Their Childhood"?

    a. to entertain the reader with a childhood story

    b. to make the reader laugh about the toy

    c. to show the reader how the boys became interested in flight

    d. to persuade the reader to experiment with flying toys

3. Under which heading would you find information about how the Wright brothers made their glider into a machine that its pilot could control?

    a. Their Childhood

    c. Achieving Their Goal

    b. Early Accomplishments

    d. Affecting the Future

4. Which of these *best* tells the central idea of this selection?

    a. The Wright brothers' first successful flight lasted only 12 seconds.

    b. The Wright brothers built upon the discoveries of other scientists.

    c. The Wright brothers were raised by parents with strong values.

    d. The Wright brothers realized the dream of human-powered flight.

5. How did the Wright brothers differ from those who had studied flight before them?

    a. They took a step-by-step approach to flying.

    b. They were interested in human flight.

    c. They had formal, scientific training in human flight.

    d. They worked with some well-known scientists.

6. Which graphic would be *most* helpful to readers trying to understand all the ideas in the selection?

    a. a line graph showing the number of motorcars and airplanes in existence during the Wright brothers' lifetime

    b. a photo of the Wright brothers at the time of their first successful flight

    c. a diagram of the Wright brothers' first plane with the parts labeled

    d. a time line showing important events in the Wright brothers' lives

© Houghton Mifflin Harcourt Publishing Company

B **Answer the question on the lines provided.**

How does the author support the viewpoint that the Wright brothers' approach to flying was better than the approach of the scientists who came before them? Use details from the selection to support your answer.

_____

_____

_____

C **Write a word to complete each sentence. Some words will not be used.**

aloft	technology	fulfillment	establish	contribution
discouraging	unreliable	manufacturer	background	

1. To set up a business or organization is to _____.

2. Something that is not dependable or trustworthy is _____.

3. All of a person's knowledge and experience is her or his _____.

4. The act of succeeding in achieving something is _____.

5. Something that causes a person to lose hope is described as _____.

6. When an object is in the air, it is _____.

7. A company that produces something, usually with machines, is a _____.

D **Is there evidence from the selection for the claims made below? On the line after each claim, write yes or no. If the answer is yes, write the number of every paragraph in which you found direct evidence.**

1. Wilbur and Orville Wright's father encouraged his sons to study the work of aircraft design.

_____

2. The Wright brothers' work in a bicycle business helped them in designing an airplane.

_____

3. After studying the work of previous aircraft designers, the Wright brothers came to believe that their design was superior.

_____

4. Wilbur usually took the lead in the Wright brothers' design work and testing.

   _____

5. The Wright brothers did not trust the work of scientists who had designed aircraft before them.

   _____

6. A result of the Wright brothers' distrust of previous scientists' data was the brothers' experimental methods, which are still being used by aviators today.

   _____

E **Think about the selections "The Wright Brothers" and "Soaring High." Answer the questions on the lines provided.**

1. Compare and contrast the two authors' viewpoints toward the Wright brothers.

   _____

   _____

   _____

2. Which author gives greater emphasis to the later effects of the Wright brothers' achievements? Give support for your answer.

   _____

   _____

   _____

   _____

F **Imagine that you have to write a report on the Wright brothers using the selections "The Wright Brothers" and "Soaring High" as sources. For each subtopic below, write *WB* if "The Wright Brothers" would be the better source. Write *SH* if "Soaring High" would be the better source.**

_____ 1. Orville and Wilbur's family life

_____ 2. Questions the Wright brothers had to answer during their early design of aircraft

_____ 3. How the Wright brothers' bicycle business influenced their design of aircraft

_____ 4. The Wright brothers' experimental methods

_____ 5. Testing models before the first flight of an airplane

_____ 6. Details of the first flight of each brother at Kitty Hawk

_____ 7. Present-day influence of the Wright brothers' achievements

34

Selection 6

Cajun Celebration

For Les and Wes Bateaux, finding something interesting to do on the weekends wasn't hard. After all, they were easy to please. There were three things they loved most. The first was their dog, Poe. The second was being outside. The third was food—any kind of food. When you live in Cajun land, Louisiana, USA, the last two are easy to find. It's jambalaya country! And Poe, well, Poe is easy to find, too. Look for the Bateaux brothers, and you'll find Poe either ahead or behind, chasing the scent of food.

Two weekends ago, the brothers and Poe decided to go to a swamp festival near their home. Poe sat with them in their pirogue, or canoe, as they paddled through alligator-infested water to their destination. Ashore, the brothers took turns tossing popcorn shrimp to Poe. Poe made the brothers proud. He'd learned to catch popcorn shrimp before he was even six months old. Now he never missed. A series of quick jaw snaps could take a pound of popcorn shrimp out of the air in minutes.

Last weekend, the brothers took Poe to a town fair. Wes and Poe ate sour, mouth-pinching pickle chips while they watched Les lose at the ring toss. Les had never been very good at ring tosses, so Wes tried. It didn't take long before Wes won a life-sized stuffed alligator. What better way to celebrate such a victory than with a plate of the beignets they loved so much? Each bite into these fried pillows of dough sent clouds of powdered sugar *poofing* into the air, some of it settling on their faces.

This weekend the brothers were in the mood for another fair. It was already Friday, and they didn't have any plans. Wes was starting to think they might have to stay at home when he heard Les drive up to the house.

35

Poe came in first, followed by Les. Both of them looked like soaked muskrats. "Whew," Les said as he took off his rain hat and hung it on a hook. Poe shook hard, sending arrows of water in every direction. "Look, Wes!" said Les, holding up a flyer. "I found one! The Frog Festival is tomorrow. Do you remember how close we came to winning the frog-racing contest last year? Let's try again this year. What do you say?"

"I don't know," said Wes. "If it's raining like this tomorrow, we may have to hop like frogs just to get there." He paused. "Heck. Let's go anyway. We'd better go down to the bayou to find a new frog."

"Yee-hah!" Les yelled and slapped his leg. "Come on, Poe. Let's go. There's nothing like a rain to bring out the frogs." Les grabbed his hat and a fishing bucket off the porch. Then he and Poe headed toward the bayou. "Come on, Wes. It's getting dark. If we're going to find a winner, we need to start now."

Saturday arrived, and the two brothers and Poe jumped into their truck. The sky didn't own a single cloud, and the air smelled of magnolia flowers and barbecue. The brothers marveled at how many people had shown up for the festival, despite yesterday's rainy weather.

Les bought the tickets while Wes asked where to sign up for the frog-racing contest. "If it's the frog-*racing* you want, you'd better hurry," said the lady selling tickets. "That contest is about to start. You'll need to sign in and get a number for your frog. The frog-*jumping* contest comes later. There's plenty of time before you have to sign up for that one."

"We want the first one," Les told the lady. "We've got a winner. I just know it."

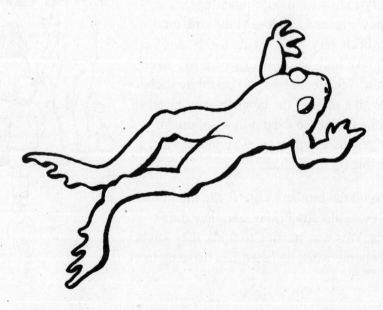

On their way to the racing grounds, the brothers and Poe passed booth after booth of spicy treats. Red pepper and other spices tickled their noses. Blackened catfish sizzled on grills. Curls of pink shrimp floated in giant soup pots. The brothers' eyes widened to take it all in. There were shelves lined with orange sweet-potato pies. There were bowls as big as kitchen sinks filled with steaming black-eyed peas, tomatoes, and okra. Tables held stacks of fried crab cakes bigger than dessert plates. There was no end to the food. The brothers were frozen with delight until Poe barked sharply. They both jumped like nervous frogs at the noise.

"We almost forgot why we're here," Wes said. "Say no more, Poe. We're on our way."

If the brothers had ever made it to the frog-racing grounds, this story would be longer. But the jambalaya got in their way. Before reaching the site for the race, the brothers passed a huge black pot sitting over an open fire. The cook stood on a ladder, stirring the thick stew with a canoe paddle. The brothers stopped to sniff. That ended their frog's chances of winning the racing contest. The smells of sweet rice, shrimp, crab, and oysters held the brothers captive. Even Poe seemed to have lost interest in the race.

"You know, Wes, surely by now that race has started, don't you think? There's no point in going over there now."

"I think you're right, Les. Poe, let's stop here a while and give our new green friend a chance to stretch his legs. He needs to warm up before the jumping contest this afternoon. Speaking of warming up, I'm ready for some jambalaya. What about you?"

"I'm more than ready," Wes said. "I don't think weekends ever can get better than this, do you?" he asked. The brothers watched Poe wag his tail and lick his lips. "See," said Wes, "even Poe agrees."

What will happen next?

Think about what you have learned about the two brothers, Wes and Les. Imagine what the brothers and Poe did the weekend after the Frog Festival. Then write a paragraph on another sheet of paper describing what they did.

A Circle the correct answer for each question.

1. Which of these is the *best* clue that the Bateaux brothers love food?

   a. Spices tickle their noses.

   c. They go places so they can eat the food there.

   b. Powdered sugar gets on their faces.

   d. They fish for food in the bayou near their house.

2. What do Les and Wes need to do at the festival before they can participate in the frog-racing contest?

   a. train the frog they found in the bayou

   c. have their frog jump in a contest

   b. test the jambalaya

   d. sign in and get a number

3. Les and Wes do not make it to the frog-racing contest because

   a. they are sidetracked by spicy food.

   c. they go to the frog-jumping contest.

   b. their dog Poe distracts them.

   d. their frog jumps too far and escapes.

4. Which of the following would be *least* important to include in a summary of the selection?

   a. At the festival, Poe, Wes, and Les pass by a pot of jambalaya cooking on a fire.

   b. Wes and Les take a frog that they found in the bayou to the festival.

   c. Poe never misses catching the popcorn shrimp he is tossed.

   d. Wes and Les live in Cajun land, which is jambalaya country.

5. Which of these phrases from the seventh paragraph *best* helps the reader understand what a *bayou* is?

   a. *fishing bucket*

   c. *getting dark*

   b. *find a winner*

   d. *nothing like a rain*

B Answer the questions on the lines provided.

1. Why does the author include the detail that Wes wins a ring toss game at the town fair?

   _____

   _____

2. Read the eleventh paragraph (about the brother and Poe passing booths of spicy treats). Explain how the author appeals to the reader's senses.

   _____

   _____

3. A moral is a message that a story gives the reader, or a lesson the reader learns from a story. What do you think would be a good moral of this selection?

   _____

   _____

C **Where in the world are Wes and Les Bateaux located? The selection and the maps will help you answer the following questions.**

1. On what continent does the selection happen? _____

2. In what country does the selection happen? _____

3. In what state does the selection happen? _____

4. How would you describe the geography of Wes and Les Bateaux's area?

   _____

5. What other phrases are used in the selection to name the area where Wes and Les live?

   _____

   _____

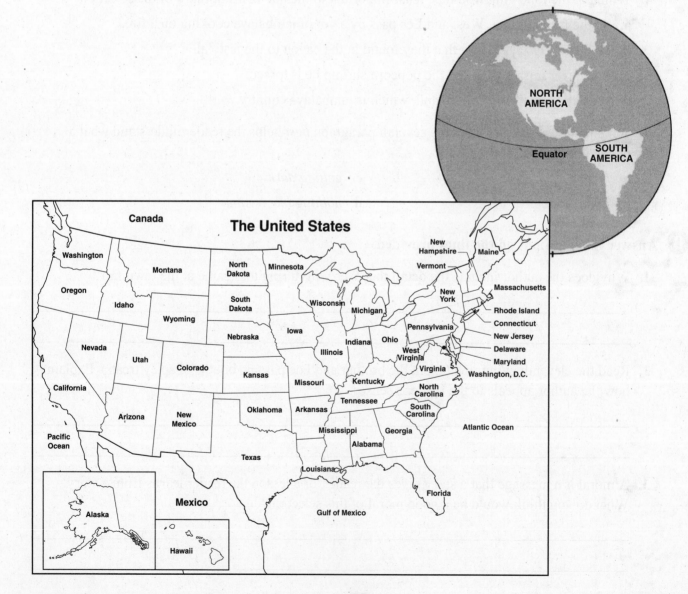

40

D **Read the following selection about frogs.**

Fascinating Frogs

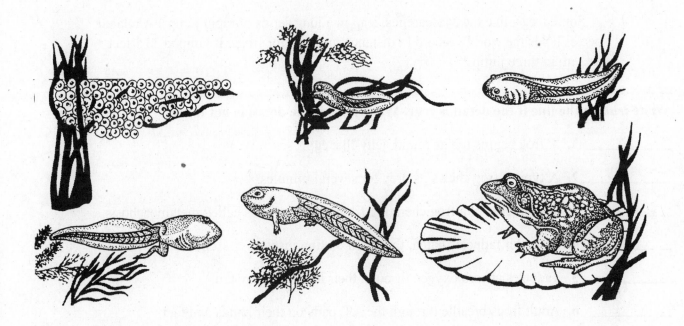

  The typical frog is a neckless, wide-mouthed, long-legged leaper. It has tiny teeth, and it cannot chew well. Its mouth must be large enough to swallow prey whole. Its hind legs are very long and strong for take-off when leaping. Its small padded front legs, or arms, take up the shock of landing.

  A frog goes through many transformations in its journey to adulthood. First, it changes from a round jelly-like egg to a tadpole with a tail and no arms or legs. This process is called *metamorphosis*, which means "changing shape."

  Most frogs lay their eggs in water. The tadpoles hatch after a few weeks, depending on the temperature. The tadpoles stay in water for a few more weeks. They swim around and feed on aquatic plants like algae. They breathe through their feathery gills, which absorb oxygen from the water.

  As the tadpole grows, many changes happen inside of its body. The gills shrink and lungs grow. The tadpole eats fewer plants and begins to feed on tiny water insects and animals. It starts to take in breaths of air using its lungs.

  As the tadpole's limbs begin to form, its tail begins to shrink and is absorbed into the body. Its legs usually start to develop first, and then the arms. Finally, the tadpole is a tiny froglet, breathing air and hunting its prey in and out of the water.

Even though all frogs have arms and legs, not all of them can leap. Some frogs walk, some crawl, and some run or hop. Certain tree frogs can even fly, or glide, from tree to tree. Almost all frogs have sticky pads on their hands and feet. They use these to cling to plants and trees.

Some frogs, like the Mascarenes, leap in a long series of rapid jumps. A related species holds the world's record in distance jumping for frogs. It jumped 33.5 feet (10.2 m) in three jumps!

Write *true* on the line if the detail is true. Write *false* if the detail is not true.

_____ 1. A frog begins life as round, jelly-like egg.

_____ 2. A typical frog chews its prey for several minutes.

_____ 3. The process of a frog changing from egg to adult is called metamorphosis.

_____ 4. Just after tadpoles hatch, they feed on tiny insects.

_____ 5. Tadpoles absorb oxygen through their long, feathery tail.

_____ 6. Adult frogs breathe through the soft pads on their hands and feet.

_____ 7. The tadpole changes into a froglet.

_____ 8. Some frogs can fly, or glide, from tree to tree.

_____ 9. Frogs have mouths that are wide enough to swallow prey whole.

_____ 10. The arms of a frog are designed to take the shock of landing.

_____ 11. Most frogs have sticky pads on their hands and feet.

_____ 12. A record-holding frog jumped 33.5 feet in one jump.

E A simile is a comparison of two things using *like* or *as*. A metaphor is a comparison of two things that are not very similar, and the words *like* and *as* are not used. Read the sentences below. Write an *M* next to each metaphor and an *S* next to each simile.

_____ 1. He bit into fried pillows of dough.

_____ 2. Clouds of powdered sugar were sent *poofing* in the air.

_____ 3. Poe and Les looked like two soaked muskrats.

_____ 4. The rainbow was a promise of better times.

_____ 5. The brothers jumped like nervous frogs at the noise.

_____ 6. The brothers were frozen with delight.

_____ 7. They were as late as yesterday.

_____ 8. The grill sizzled and sounded like rain.

_____ 9. Poe shook hard, sending arrows of water in every direction.

_____ 10. Alligators swam just below the surface like bumpy submarines.

F The author of "Cajun Celebration" uses some unusual words like *pirogue* and *jambalaya*. These words, although a part of English usage, have their beginnings in other cultures. Use your dictionary or Internet skills to look up the words below. On the line next to each word, write the country or culture where the word began and the word's definition. One has been done for you.

1. Cajun *Acadian French—a native of Louisiana* _____

2. pirogue _____

3. beignet _____

4. jambalaya _____

5. barbecue _____

6. bayou _____

7. festival _____

8. okra _____

Selection 7

A Law of Motion

Sir Isaac Newton was an English mathematician and scientist who lived in the 1600s and 1700s. He published his three laws of motion, which describe how forces affect the motion of an object, in 1687. You can demonstrate one of Newton's laws of motion with an apparatus called a Newton's cradle. The cradle will show that things at rest tend to stay at rest until acted on by an outside force. A Newton's cradle also demonstrates what scientists call the "Principle of Conservation of Energy." This means that energy is never created or destroyed. Energy can change from one form to another, but the total amount of energy stays the same.

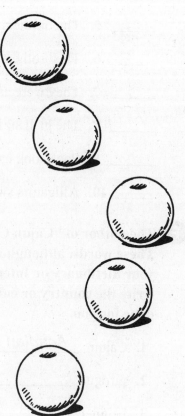

It is easier to understand these scientific principles if you use your own Newton's cradle. You need only a few materials to build one.

• 1 ruler marked in inches

• 1 pencil or dowel rod

• scissors

• 5 paper clips

• 5 8-in. pieces of fishing line

• 5 wooden beads

Once you have your materials, you are ready to begin building your Newton's cradle. Here's how.

First, use your ruler to make five marks on the pencil or dowel rod. The marks should be exactly one inch apart. Be sure the third mark is in the center of the pencil or dowel rod.

Second, use the scissors to score, or cut, a ring around each mark on the pencil or dowel rod. The ring should go all the way around the pencil or rod. Handle the scissors carefully so that you do not cut your skin.

Third, tie a paper clip to one end of each piece of fishing line. Place each paper clip in exactly the same place on each line.

Fourth, thread one piece of fishing line through the hole in each bead. Each bead will rest on a paper clip.

Fifth, tie each piece of fishing line around the scored rings on the pencil or dowel rod. The beads must line up exactly and hang evenly.

Use one hand to hold the pencil or rod horizontally. Pull the first bead on one end back. Then release it gently. Observe what happens. The bead you release exerts a force on the other beads.

Now consider the Principle of Conservation of Energy to examine what happens to the beads on your Newton's cradle. Before you released the bead, the bead had one kind of energy called potential energy. When you let the bead fall, the potential energy changed into another kind of energy called kinetic energy. Kinetic energy is the energy of motion.

Wait. There are still more transformations in energy. When the first bead hit the second bead, what did you hear? You heard a click. A click is sound energy. Now think about what happens when two things rub together. For example, if you rub your hands together, can you feel your hands getting warmer? The kinetic energy in your hands changes to heat energy. The same thing happens with the beads on your Newton's cradle. As the first bead hits the second bead, energy moves through the beads to the bead at the other end. The bead lifts, swings back, and hits the line of beads. Each time a bead hits another bead, kinetic energy changes to sound and heat energy. Eventually, the kinetic energy changes completely to sound and heat, and the beads stop moving. But don't expect this to happen quickly. Since the changes of energy are small, it takes some time for the beads to stop moving.

Now you know how to build a Newton's cradle. You also know how to use the cradle to demonstrate some interesting scientific principles. Try making other Newton's cradles. Use different sizes of dowel rods and string. Change the number of beads, or use metal beads. You might even want to demonstrate your super science skills in front of a group of people.

A Circle the correct answer for each question.

1. A Newton's cradle demonstrates that things stay at rest unless acted on by an

   a. inside force.   **c.** outside force.

   b. energetic force.   **d.** overhead force.

2. Although energy can change form, the total amount of energy

   a. grows stronger.   **c.** slowly disappears.

   b. decreases in strength.   **d.** stays the same.

3. The energy of a bead in a Newton's cradle changes from potential energy into kinetic energy because

   a. the bead is in motion as it falls.   **c.** the bead makes a clicking sound.

   b. the bead releases energy.   **d.** the bead was hanging evenly with the other beads.

4. Read this sentence from the eleventh paragraph.

   > **There are still more transformations in energy.**

   Which word in the tenth paragraph *best* helps the reader understand what "transformations" means?

   a. *examine*   **c.** *happens*

   b. *released*   **d.** *changed*

5. Read this detail from the eleventh paragraph.

   > **Each time a bead hits another bead, kinetic energy changes to sound and heat energy.**

   Which of these statements from the selection does this detail *best* support?

   a. *Energy can change from one form to another, but the total amount of energy stays the same.*

   b. *The cradle will show that things at rest tend to stay at rest until acted on by an outside force.*

   c. *This means that energy is never created or destroyed.*

   d. *Since the changes of energy are small, it takes some time for the beads to stop moving.*

6. What is the eleventh paragraph *mainly* about?

   a. how kinetic energy can change to heat energy in certain circumstances

   b. how energy changes when a Newton's cradle is in motion

   c. how the beads on a Newton's cradle move when the apparatus is set in motion

   d. how changes in energy happen all the time, but slowly and gradually

B "A Law of Motion" is an example of a how-to paper. A how-to paper usually explains steps in a process. The steps in the process must be done in sequence in order to make sense. Number the sections of this selection to form a correct sequence of events. One section is done for you.

A Scientist at Work in the Rain Forest

_____1_____ You have always wanted to discover a new species of plant. You decide to travel to the rain forest in Brazil to conduct a detailed search of the flora.

_____ Your assistants carefully dig up plant specimens. They bag them and number them. The plants are gently carried back to camp.

_____ Your flight is uneventful. After reaching Brazil, you hire assistants and buy supplies.

_____ Behind the waterfall, you find several species of plants that you have never seen before. It will take you a long time to carefully catalog each species and research it.

_____ Before your flight, you must gather digging tools, cameras, books, maps, and other equipment. You must apply for permission from the Brazilian government to remove specimens from the rain forest.

_____ When you fly out over the rain forest, you are sad. You wonder what other discoveries are hiding in the jungle waiting to be found. You turn your thoughts to the new plant species in the plane's cargo hold and your journey home.

_____ You show the assistants how to use the special digging tools. You show them how to wrap the roots of any plants that you might find to prepare them for transport.

_____ Finally, you make a very exciting discovery—a waterfall! The assistants help you find a way into the cave behind the spray of water. Something interesting catches your eye.

_____ At last, you decide you have taken enough specimens. It is time to return home. The plants are packed up. Soon, you will be flying back to your own country.

Name _____ Date _____

C Synonyms are words that mean the same or almost the same. Circle the two synonyms on each line.

1.	bleached	blackened	cruel	darkened
2.	ancient	potential	experienced	possible
3.	exert	apply	discard	prepare
4.	discover	show	hide	demonstrate
5.	underneath	distant	outside	exterior
6.	emerge	retreat	appear	fade
7.	attract	continue	reveal	sustain
8.	dispute	participate	oppose	survive
9.	industrious	subdued	panicked	hardworking
10.	rebellion	dismay	protest	celebration
11.	theory	menu	degree	idea

D Choose a word from below to complete each sentence. Some words will not be used.

flora	apparatus	principle
specimen	conserve	demonstrate
species	catalog	dowel
cargo	kinetic energy	specific

1. An instrument or tool is an _____.

2. The plants in a location are the _____.

3. A sample from a group for scientific study is a _____.

4. A group of similar organisms is a _____.

5. A rule or law is a _____.

6. To make an organized list of items is to _____.

7. The energy of motion is _____.

8. A long, wooden rod is called a _____.

9. A load carried by a plane or a ship is called _____.

10. To show how something works is to _____.

E Another of Newton's laws says that "for every reaction there is an equal and opposite reaction." This could be called the law of cause and effect. It means that for every action there is a result, or consequence. Read the following how-to paper and think about causes and effects.

The Color of Light

Nearly 300 years ago in England, Sir Isaac sat by his study window on a rare, sunny day. The sunlight played over the prism, a triangular piece of glass, he held in his hand. The sparkling colored light danced on the walls of his study. He noticed that when the rays of the sun, called white light, passed through the prism, the colors of the rainbow could be seen.

This made him curious. Sir Isaac was always feeling curious. When an apple had fallen on his head, it made him wonder about the force pulling on the falling apple. This led him to his theory about gravity. Now he was curious about the colored light he saw emerging from the prism.

Sir Isaac knew that a current theory stated that the thickness of a prism changed the actual color of light when it passed through a prism. However, he had a different idea. He thought that a prism *separated* the colors already present in white light.

Sir Isaac decided to repeat the prism experiment. Every time he conducted it, he saw that the resulting "rainbow" light always appeared in the same order. The colors produced—red, orange, yellow, green, blue, indigo (blue violet), and violet—always maintained the same order every time he passed white light through the prism. Sir Isaac noticed that when a second prism was used, the rainbow of colors could be changed back into white light.

Unlike sound waves, light waves do not need a substance to travel through. They can travel through the emptiness of space. Ordinary sunlight, called white light, has waves of many different lengths. Each color has its own wavelength. When white light passes through a prism, each color of light bends at a specific angle. As a result, the colors leaving the prism always keep the same order. Red is the color with the longest wavelength, so it is the top band on the rainbow. Violet has the shortest wavelength, so it is the bottom band on the rainbow.

Light passing through water or raindrops in the atmosphere can create a rainbow in the sky. The drops act like little prisms bending white light and separating it into the different colors.

Sir Isaac's theory of light and color was a new one. Many scientists of his day were angry with him. They did not agree with his theory. He eventually grew tired of the argument and wrote a letter saying he was sorry he had ever put forth his idea.

Match the correct effect to its cause. Look back through the selection. Write the letter of the effect beside its cause.

CAUSE	EFFECT

_____ 1. Colored light danced on Newton's study wall and

a. emerged from the prism in a rainbow of colors.

_____ 2. An apple falling made Newton wonder and

b. the colored light blended back into white light.

_____ 3. Newton noticed that white light going into a prism

c. can create a rainbow in the sky.

_____ 4. When Newton repeated the prism experiment,

d. it discouraged Newton, and he wrote a letter of regret.

_____ 5. When Newton used a second prism on the rainbow light,

e. led him to his theory about the force called gravity.

_____ 6. Because red has the longest wavelength,

f. it emerges as the top band of color.

_____ 7. Because violet has the shortest wavelength,

g. he noticed that the colors always kept the same order.

_____ 8. Light passing through raindrops

h. made him curious.

_____ 9. When other scientists argued with Newton's light theory,

i. it emerges as the bottom band of color.

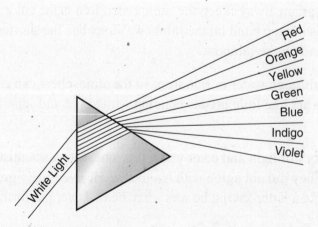

Red
Orange
Yellow
Green
Blue
Indigo
Violet

White Light

50

Skills Review: Selections 1–7

A Read the selection below. Note the details. Underline the main idea, or topic sentence, in each paragraph. Then circle the correct answers to the questions that follow.

1   Most chameleons live in the rain forest where the climate is warm and rainy. However, chameleons live in many different habitats all over the continent of Africa and on the island country of Madagascar just off the coast of Africa. They can even live in the dry sands of the desert or in higher elevations in the mountains.

2   There are many different kinds of trees and plants in the rain forest that provide food and shelter for chameleons. The trees, vines, and other plants grow close together, giving the chameleon many places to hide from predators. The rain forest is ideal for chameleons.

3   Chameleons are reptiles, or cold-blooded crawling animals. A reptile's body warms or cools to about the same temperature as the air or water around it. The mild, or temperate, moist climate of the rain forest is suited to the needs of the chameleon's body.

4   Chameleons are also lizards, but they differ from other lizards in a few ways. Chameleons cannot grow new tails if they are injured like other lizards do. Chameleons also move more slowly than most lizards.

5   Chameleons have bulging, heavy-lidded eyes that are unique. Chameleons can move each of their eyes in a different direction. One eye can look forward while the other looks backward. This is handy for spying and catching prey.

6   Sunlight, temperature, and mood make some chameleons change their color. This special color-changing feature makes chameleons of interest to scientists. Scientists have found that chameleons do not use their color-changing ability to hide. It is the chameleon's normal color that provides them with camouflage.

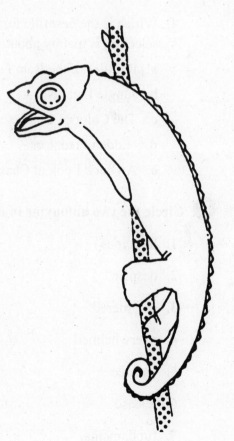

1. Which paragraph tells about some features of a chameleon's eyes?

   a. paragraph 4   b. paragraph 5   c. paragraph 3

2. What is paragraph 2 *mainly* about?

   a. which animals seek food and shelter in the rain forest

   b. where chameleons hide from predators

   c. why the plants of the rain forest grow close together

   d. why the rain forest is a good place for chameleons to live

3. What is paragraph 4 *mainly* about?

   a. Chameleons differ from other lizards.

   b. Chameleons cannot grow new tails.

   c. Chameleons are lizards.

   d. Chameleons move more slowly than other lizards.

4. Which is the *best* title for the selection? Remember that the title should tell what the selection is mainly about.

   a. Reptiles of the Rain Forest

   b. Jungle Lizards

   c. The Color of Chameleons

   d. Hidden Predators

   e. A Quick Look at Chameleons

B **Circle the two antonyms in each group of words below.**

1. ferocious	trapped	tame	endangered
2. despise	resist	join	disable
3. disordered	expelled	exposed	camouflaged
4. overwhelmed	regulated	established	uncontrolled
5. enforce	enlist	resign	justify
6. release	seize	stalk	explore
7. fundamental	actual	potential	fantasy

Name _____ Date _____

C Read the selection and write a summary of it on the lines below. Then go back to the selection and underline the sentences that are statements of opinion.

What Happened to the Maya?

No one is certain about what caused the great Mayan civilization to begin fading. Around AD 900, the Maya stopped carving the standing stones, called stelae, on which they recorded their history. There is evidence that many Maya began leaving their cities at this time. The rain forest grew over the ruins of the Mayan stone temples and buildings. It is sad that such an advanced culture is no more.

In 1238, the Maya living in the Yucatan moved their capital city from Chichen Itza to Mayapan. They built Mayapan with a thick stone wall surrounding it to protect the city from enemies. Perhaps the Maya were looking for some peace after all their troubles.

In the 1500s, the Spanish conquistadors came to Mesoamerica. They wanted to find gold and riches to take back to Spain. Gold is difficult for everyone to resist since it is so beautiful. The Spanish found about sixty Mayan cities and began to conquer them. Some were taken easily. In other cities, the Maya fought in ferocious battles and repulsed the Spanish invaders.

The Maya who lived in the Yucatan peninsula refused to surrender. They fought against the Spanish for twenty years. The Spanish made some of them slaves. Others were converted to Spanish beliefs. The Spanish destroyed Mayan art and books to keep the Maya under control. One group of Maya, the Itza, stayed free until 1697. When Mexico became its own country in 1821, the Maya tried to take back their land several times without success.

_____

_____

_____

_____

_____

_____

_____

_____

_____

53

D **A reader can gain clues about a character from what he or she says, thinks, and does—as well as from things that other characters think and say about him or her. Read the following excerpt from a selection. Underline the parts of the excerpt that give you clues about the character named Lana. Then, on the lines provided, write a paragraph about the type of person Lana is.**

Lana heard a soft knock on her door. She scowled. "Why can't I ever have time to myself?" she thought. It had been a rough week. Too many tests and deadlines. Too many complicated friendships. Too many nights with too little sleep. She was just about to yell *go away* when she made the connection: The only person in the world who knocked like that—like a timid mouse—was her nephew Tommy. And Tommy was so cute, so cuddly, so uncomplicated that he was like an antidote to her snakebite life.

She opened the door and looked down, expecting to see the four-year-old's smiling face. But she saw black leggings instead. She raised her head. "Jenna, what are you doing here?"

Jenna's eyes were puffy from crying. "I'm here because you're my friend." A few quiet sobs escaped her. "And I need your advice. And you give better advice than anyone I know."

Lana took a quick glance behind her—one of almost longing—at the drawing pad she'd left on the floor. Then, after letting out a sigh, she said to Jenna, "What happened?"

_____

_____

_____

_____

_____

_____

_____

_____

_____

_____

_____

Name _____ Date _____

Study the information in the table. Then answer the questions below.

Weather in Degrees (Fahrenheit)

State	City	Yesterday	Today
Ala.	Birmingham	89/69	85/68
	Mobile	93/72	91/72
Alaska	Anchorage	57/48	61/45
	Fairbanks	56/42	56/42
Ariz.	Phoenix	101/77	101/77
	Tucson	95/69	97/72
Ark.	Little Rock	78/66	71/61
Calif.	Los Angeles	85/62	85/66
	San Francisco	73/54	81/56
Colo.	Aspen	55/37	67/37
	Denver	59/33	68/44

1. Which of the following information does this table contain?

   a. rainfall in different states

   b. high and low temperatures in different states

   c. humidity in different states

   d. the daily ozone measure in different states

2. Based on the information in the table, the figures listed are *most likely* for a day in which month?

   a. September   c. December

   b. January   d. February

3. Which city has the highest temperature today?

   a. Phoenix   c. Birmingham

   b. Tucson   d. Los Angeles

4. In the table, which two cities have the greatest difference in temperature?

   a. Mobile and Tucson   c. Phoenix and Aspen

   b. Fairbanks and Denver   d. Little Rock and San Francisco

Selection 8

Two Sports for Skaters

Two fast-moving sports popular with vigorous people of all ages are two kinds of skating. They are in-line skating and ice-skating. Whether skaters are on the sidewalk or on the ice, most of them can enjoy hours of fun. That is, of course, if they are limber and have the right equipment.

Skaters in both sports use equipment that is alike and different. Both kinds of skates are made for speed. Today's skates let a skater skate well all the time. Skaters can also use their skates in more than one sport. However, certain kinds of skates are made for different uses. They work best when a skater uses the right skate for the right sport. This means, for example, that a hockey player uses skates made for hockey. She can also use them to figure skate. However, in that case, she will probably skate better if she uses skates made for figure skating.

All in-line skates are made for land. So they all have the same fundamental features. An in-line skate has a boot that is usually made from plastic. Because the boot is firm, it holds the skater's ankles comfortably. The boot's lining comes out so it can be washed. On the outside of the boot, there are laces, buckles, or both to fasten the boot.

Ice skates also have a boot, but it is made only for ice. The boot is usually made from leather. It provides support for the ankles. It is also designed to be comfortable and warm. The boot's lining is made from a material that helps air move. However, the longer the skater wears the boot, the more likely the person's feet will perspire. Over time, this can cause a boot to deteriorate, or break down. This possibility of deterioration makes it important to wipe out the boot after each use.

Both kinds of skates have one or more objects that help the skater move. In-line skates use wheels—usually four. There are three things about the wheels that require the skater's attention: size, hardness, and bearings. To check the size of the wheel, the skater measures the wheel's diameter in millimeters (mm). The size of the wheel is important, because the larger it is, the faster it rolls. Most ordinary in-line skates range from approximately 72 mm to 76 mm. The size is marked on the side of the wheel.

The second important feature of the wheel is its hardness. Wheels are made from a kind of plastic. The hardness of the plastic varies and is measured in durometers. A zero durometer represents the softest plastic. One hundred durometers represents the hardest plastic. The harder the plastic that the wheel is made of, the faster the skater can go.

The last important feature of a wheel is its bearings. Bearings are fundamental to the way in-line skates work. Ball bearings are inside the hubs of the wheels. These ball bearings let the wheels roll. So, the better the ball bearings, the faster the wheels roll. Good ball bearings mean that a skater will get more mileage out of his or her skates as well.

Instead of wheels, ice skates use blades. The blades are attached to the soles of the boot with a screw mount. This mount holds the blade tightly in place. Blades are made of metal, usually stainless steel. Then they are coated with another metal, such as chrome, nickel, or aluminum. The blade is solid and has a toe pick at the front end. The toe pick lets the skater grip the ice. It also helps the skater take off. A ridge runs along the bottom of the blade. This ridge is called the "hollow." The hollow cuts the ice as the skater glides over it.

Being able to come to an abrupt stop is important to every skater. Only in-line skates have brakes. Brake pads are attached to the back of each boot. The skater stops by lifting his or her toes and pressing the brake pad to the ground.

For ice skaters, stopping is another matter. There are no brakes on ice skates. Instead, skaters use their legs and feet to stop, pressing on the sides of their skates.

In-line skating and ice-skating are alike in some ways and different in others. Their differences make both sports interesting to many skaters. The ways they are alike let skaters skate in both sports. For ambitious skaters with the right skates, skating is several sports in one.

What will happen next?

Think about what you have learned about in-line skating and ice-skating. Write a paragraph on another sheet of paper telling what you think the next major development in skating might be.

Ⓐ Circle the correct answer for each question.

1. What was probably the author's *main* purpose for writing the selection?

   a. to describe sports that vigorous and ambitious athletes like

   b. to compare metal blades and plastic wheels

   c. to comment on sports that are popular in different seasons

   d. to compare in-line skates and ice skates

2. Skates work the best when

   a. they are worn for a long time. **c.** there is low humidity and less friction.

   b. they are worn mostly in cold weather. **d.** the correct skate is chosen for the sport.

3. Instead of wheels, ice skates have

    a. bearings.   **c.** a plastic lining.

    b. blades.   **d.** brake pads.

4. The toe pick on the blades of ice skates helps a skater

    a. glide over the ice.   **c.** grip the ice.

    b. choose a direction to skate in.   **d.** clean the ice off the toe of the boot.

5. Read this sentence from the sixth paragraph.

> **A zero durometer represents the softest plastic.**

Which word in the sixth paragraph **best** helps the reader understand what "durometer" means?

    a. *varies*   **b.** *hardness*   **c.** *feature*   **d.** *hundred*

6. Read this detail from the fifth paragraph.

> **Both kinds of skates have one or more objects that help the skater move.**

Which of these statements from the selection does this detail **best** support?

    a. *The boot is usually made of leather.*

    b. *Today's skates let a skater skate well all the time.*

    c. *Being able to come to an abrupt stop is important to every skater.*

    d. *The harder the plastic that the wheel is made of, the faster the skater can go.*

7. Which paragraph provides the **best** support for how the author feels about in-line skating and ice skating?

    a. paragraph 1   **c.** paragraph 9

    b. paragraph 2   **d.** paragraph 11

B   **Answer the question on the lines provided.**

Explain how the author organizes the selection.

_____

_____

_____

C Outlining is a method of organizing by making an ordered list to show how ideas are related. To outline:

    1. Use Roman numerals (I, II, III) to list the main idea groups.
    2. Use capital letters (A, B, C) to list supporting ideas.
    3. Use Arabic numerals (1, 2, 3) to list details and examples.

Use the outline below to collect research for a speech about how in-line skates and ice skates are alike and different. Use the selection about skates to complete the outline.

In-line Skates and Ice Skates

I. How in-line skates and ice skates are alike

  A. Features of the skates that are alike

    1. Both are built for speed.

    2. _____

    3. _____

  B. Parts of the skates that are alike

    1. _____

    2. Both have devices that help the skater move.

II. How in-line skates and ice skates are different

  A. Features of the skates that are different

    1. In-line skates are designed for use on land, ice skates for ice.

    2. _____

    3. _____

  B. Parts of the skates that are different

    1. _____

    2. _____

  C. How in-line skates and ice skates stop

    1. _____

    2. _____

Name _____ Date _____

D Compare the information in the two circle graphs below and answer the questions.

Skaters in the United States

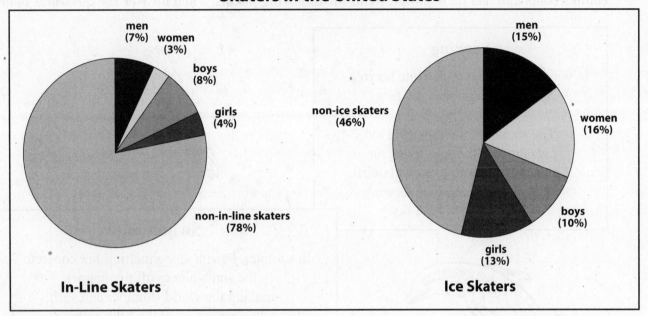

In-Line Skaters   **Ice Skaters**

1. What percentage of in-line skaters are men?

   a. 13 percent   **c.** 15 percent

   b. 7 percent   **d.** 10 percent

2. What percentage of ice skaters are women?

   a. 4 percent   **c.** 13 percent

   b. 20 percent   **d.** 16 percent

3. Based on the circle graphs, which statement below is true?

   a. Fewer women than girls ice skate.

   b. More men than women in-line skate.

   c. More girls than boys in-line skate.

   d. Of all the ice skaters, 15% are children.

4. What percentage of ice skaters are adult males?

   a. 7 percent   **c.** 8 percent

   b. 10 percent   **d.** 15 percent

5. An informal survey of skaters shows that there are more ice skaters than in-line skaters in the United States. Why do you think that is the case?

   _____

   _____

Most poets make comparisons in their work. Often the comparisons are not stated as they would be in "ordinary talk." You have to stay with the poem for a while to understand the comparisons and feel their power. Read the following poems. Then answer the questions below.

Soaring

In winter, I fly across the white horizon—
the cold wind bites my face
and traces my flight.
The sound of blades slicing ice
cuts through the splintering air.
I'm full of graceful spins and twirls
like a falcon turning on its wing
high in a crisp blue sky.

Swimming

In summer, I swim along melting-hot concrete—
the sun bounces off my helmet,
making the world shimmer and shift.
Wheels whine in the heat, singing
and clicking like a dolphin.
I jump and pump my lazy legs
left right, left right, left right
through a sea of yellow hazy heat.

1. What is the poet comparing to flying like a falcon in "Soaring"?

_____

2. What is the poet comparing to swimming "along melting-hot concrete" in "Swimming"?

_____

3. What do the comparisons in "Soaring" tell you about the weather?

_____

_____

4. How does the poet compare the sound of her wheels to a dolphin in "Swimming"?

_____

5. Why do you think the world shimmers and shifts in the poem "Swimming"?

_____

F There are different ways you can compare one thing to another. One way is to compare pairs of things to each other. This type of comparison is called an analogy. When doing this, think about how the first two things—that is, the things in the first pair of words—are related to each other. Then apply how these things are related to the two things in the second pair of words. Complete each sentence by circling the correct word.

Examples:

a. *Rectangle* is to *swimming pool* as *circle* is to *wheel*.
   (A swimming pool is a rectangle, and a wheel is a circle.)

b. *Boot* is to *foot* as *hat* is to *head*.
   (You wear a boot on your foot. You wear a hat on your head.)

c. *Artist* is to *painting* as *musician* is to _____. (All the words are alike because they deal with artistic activities. Which word that expresses an artistic activity would fit in the comparison and make sense?)

   gardening   (music)   training

1. *Silver* is to *metal* as *silk* is to _____.
   plastic   wood   fabric

2. *Freezing* is to *melting* as *uniting* is to _____.
   joining   meeting   splintering

3. *Hard* is to *soft* as *stiff* is to _____.
   asleep   limber   bored

4. *Singing* is to *music* as *skating* is to _____.
   sports   cooking   ice rinks

5. *Bicycle chains* are to *bike wheels* as *bearings* are to _____.
   durometers   skate wheels   ice-skate blades

6. *Building* is to *square footage* as *trip* is to _____.
   inches   durometers   mileage

7. *Cold* is to *chills* as *heat* is to _____.
   perspiration   exercise   thermometer

8. *Sadness* is to *tears* as *teasing* is to _____.
   love   laziness   embarrassment

9. *Painting* is to *canvas* as *writing* is to _____.
   paper   · encyclopedia   desk

G Find a word from below that is a synonym for the underlined word in each sentence. Then write each sentence using the new word. One word will not be used.

approximate	deteriorate	ambitious
fundamentals	abruptly	limber

1. The measurement was <u>close</u>, but not exact.

   _____

2. Because she is <u>motivated</u>, she wants to make the Honor's List.

   _____

3. The green leaves fell in the pond water and began to <u>rot</u>.

   _____

4. He had missed out on the <u>basics</u> of algebra and was behind in the class.

   _____

5. She is a dancer and is very <u>flexible</u>.

   _____

H Write all the words from below that mean the same or almost the same as *vigorous*. Some words will not be used.

tireless	heroic	brilliant
spirited	energetic	unfailing
gallant	panicked	strong
cowardly	strenuous	unweary
lively	talented	bashful

1. _____   5. _____

2. _____   6. _____

3. _____   7. _____

4. _____   8. _____

Selection 9

A Look at Salt and Spices

Chances are, you don't give much thought to salt when you sprinkle it on popcorn—or to cinnamon or other spices when you use them to slightly change the flavor of a food. Nevertheless, throughout history people have worked for, fought for, and made and spent fortunes for some specific substances that we use today to season food—namely, salt, which is a mineral, and pepper and saffron, which are spices.

Let's look at ordinary table salt first. Salt is found in seawater, in salt wells, and beneath the ground. Some type of heat energy is needed to remove salt from seawater. Large pools of water can be left in the sun. Also, large pans of salt water, called dryers, can be placed over fires. In either case, the water evaporates and leaves the salt behind.

A salt well is like an oil well. Two pipes, one inside the other, are drilled into the ground. Fresh water is pumped down. Salt in the soil dissolves in the water. As more fresh water is forced down, the salt water is forced up. Once it's on the surface, the water is treated like ocean water. That is, it's heated until it evaporates and leaves the salt behind.

Salt is also part of rocks almost everywhere around the world. People dig mines beneath the ground and use machines to break the rock salt apart and bring it to the surface. It's crushed to different sizes and bagged or boxed for consumers. In our hands or on our food, salt is a grainy, white substance with no scent.

Salt has a long history. Even in ancient times, people used salt for different purposes, including seasoning and preserving their food. About 3000 BC, Chinese people wrote about salt in their books of medicine. In ancient Egypt, salt was used to preserve dead bodies. In ancient Rome, soldiers were paid in salt. Some say the word *soldier* comes from the words *sal dare*, which mean "to give salt." Salt was once pressed into coins more valuable than gold. Motivated by its value, people fought wars and traveled far to find and control it.

Pepper is an important spice. Unlike salt, pepper begins as a berry. Pepper plants are shrubs that climb like vines or trail across the ground. They grow where it's hot, such as in Indonesia. Pepper plants form small green berries about the size of a pea. As the berries ripen, they turn red. When they change color, the berries are picked, cleaned, and dried. Whether they bake in the sun or over fires, as they heat, the berries turn black. Then they're ground to make a powder. The powder may be black, white, or red, depending on the kind of pepper plant that made the berries and the process used to make the pepper. No matter the color, pepper has a scent and sharp taste that makes it easy to identify.

In the early days of trade between Europe and India, pepper was so expensive that it was reserved for royalty. A king or queen might receive a few pounds of pepper as a gift. One king, named Alaric I, is said to have demanded pepper to stop his attack on Rome in AD 408. Hippocrates, the father of medicine, thought pepper helped the heart and kidneys work. Even today, some people use pepper as a medicine.

Saffron is another spice with an interesting history. It comes from the female parts of the purple saffron crocus, a flower. Each flower must be picked by hand in the autumn when the flowers are fully open. It may take up to 250,000 flowers to make one pound of saffron. Now you can understand why saffron is one of the most expensive spices in the world. This spice is sold in the form of a yellow-orange powder or as slender red threads. Most of the world's saffron crocus flowers are grown in India, Iran, and Spain.

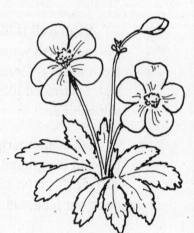

Like salt and pepper, saffron is used to season foods such as rice. It's also used as medicine. In India, hosts give their guests food flavored with saffron as a sign of honor. People also use saffron to treat or prevent diseases such as the common cold.

Records show that people in ancient Egypt and Rome around 27 BC used saffron as a dye for cloth. They also used it to make perfumes and medicines and to season food. Traders carried the spice through Asia, and in time, through Europe. Because the spice was expensive, people used it as a sign of their wealth and power. In the early 1500s, the ladies in the court of King Henry VIII, for example, used saffron to dye their hair.

The next time you salt or pepper a food, or you see someone cooking with saffron or some other spice, you'll know that it carries with it more than meets the eye—or the tongue.

What would your imaginary feast be?

What are your favorite spices and seasonings? If you were on a desert island, what meal would you daydream about? Write a brief paragraph on another sheet of paper describing your imaginary feast. Make sure you name the spices and seasonings used to prepare the foods.

A **Circle the correct answer for each question.**

1. According to the selection, ancient Chinese people used salt to

   a. pay soldiers.

   b. preserve dead bodies.

   c. treat diseases.

   d. make coins.

2. What are pepper plants?

   a. fruits

   b. flowers

   c. trees

   d. shrubs

3. People in ancient Egypt used saffron for all of the following *except*

   a. to pay soldiers.

   b. in perfumes.

   c. as a medicine.

   d. as a dye.

4. What are the second, third, and fourth paragraphs *mainly* about?

   a. what the role of heat is in the removal of salt

   b. how salt varies according to where it came from

   c. why salt is so difficult to find in nature

   d. how salt is taken from sources in nature

5. Read this sentence from the third paragraph.

   ┌───┐
   │ **Salt in the soil dissolves in the water.**   │
   └───┘

   The word *dissolves* indicates that the salt

   a. gets hotter as it rises from the well.

   b. becomes part of the liquid it is in.

   c. evaporates as if it were in ocean water.

   d. is forced up from below the ground.

B **Answer the questions on the lines provided.**

1. Based on the selection, why do you think at earlier times in history people spent a fortune to obtain spices?

_____

_____

_____

2. What is the author's point of view toward salt and spices?

_____

_____

_____

© Houghton Mifflin Harcourt Publishing Company

Selection 9

Core Skills Reading Comprehension, Grade 7

C Use the outline that follows to organize your thoughts for a paper you have been assigned on salt and spices. Use the selection titled "A Look at Salt and Spices" and the two boxes below titled "Additional Information" to complete the outline. Only use *relevant* information.

Additional Information

Mohandas K. Gandhi was a leader of the Indian struggle for independence from Britain. People called him Mahatma, which means "great soul." He believed that it is wrong to hurt another person. He thought that the best way to make the British leave India was for people to refuse to obey unfair laws. He called this passive, or peaceful, resistance.

When the British put a tax on salt that made it too costly for poor Indians, he decided he would walk to the sea and produce salt himself. In 1930, he started to walk the 150-mile distance. Along the way, people saw what he was doing and followed him. Thousands joined him in his march to the sea. When they saw their own strength in numbers, the Indian people began to resist the British in a series of nonviolent protests. These protests succeeded in ridding India of British rule in 1947.

Gandhi's ideas about nonviolence have influenced many people and world leaders. Dr. Martin Luther King, Jr., successfully used Gandhi's methods in the civil rights movement in the United States.

Additional Information

Spices have been produced in India for thousands of years. Throughout history, people from other regions of the world have taken spices from there, either through trade or by force. The ancient Romans had early contact with India and traded for salt and other spices.

Arab traders first began invading India in the AD 600s. Later the Europeans began to move into India. The Portugese explorer Vasco da Gama challenged Arab control of the spice trade with India in 1498. His ship was met with Indian gunfire and a blockade in an Indian harbor.

In the 1600s, Queen Elizabeth I, the sovereign of Britain, sent a group of traders to India. The British East India Company managed to gain power by signing treaties and forcing alliances with different Indian princes. The British were well positioned to gain power in India. In the eighteenth century, they controlled the spice trade.

Salt and Spices

I. Three important food seasonings

   A. Salt

      1. Found in seawater, salt wells, and under the ground

      2. A white, grainy mineral with no scent

   B. _____

      1. _____

      2. White, red, or black powder

   C. Saffron

      1. _____

      2. _____

      3. _____

      4. _____

II. Purpose and value

   A. Salt

      1. _____

      2. _____

      3. _____

      4. _____

      5. _____

   B. Pepper

      1. _____

      2. _____

   C. _____

      1. _____

      2. _____

      3. _____

      4. _____

      5. _____

      6. _____

      7. _____

III. India as a source of spices

    A. Ancient Roman traders in India

    B. Arab traders in India in AD 600s

    C. _____

    D. _____

        1. _____

        2. _____

        3. _____

IV. A more recent struggle over salt

    A. _____

    B. _____

D   **Write a word from below to complete each sentence.**

blockade	passive	season
evaporates	nonviolent	alliance
resistance	preserve	sovereign

1. The opposite of *aggressive* is _____.

2. The highest ruler in the land is a _____.

3. To be peaceful and not fight is to be _____.

4. When water dries into the atmosphere, it _____.

5. To add flavor to foods is to _____.

6. To prevent something from going bad is to _____.

7. A union between groups is an _____.

8. An obstacle to prevent a ship from passing into a port is a _____.

9. An act of opposition is a _____.

E Choose words from below to solve the crossword puzzle.

Egypt	*sal dare*	crocus
trial	pepper	opens
lesson	daisies	shrub
skate	blockades	dryers
preserves	unless	saffron
China	royalty	salt

Across

1. Ancient Roman words that mean "to give salt"
3. a spice that is a powder made from dried berries
4. a small, bushy plant
6. the opposite of *shuts*
8. a boot with a blade mounted on it
10. where saffron was used to dye cloth
11. small flowers
12. a food seasoning that comes from seawater

Down

2. salt pans set out in the sun
5. obstacles in a road or outside a port
7. a word that means "except"
9. a judge conducts this

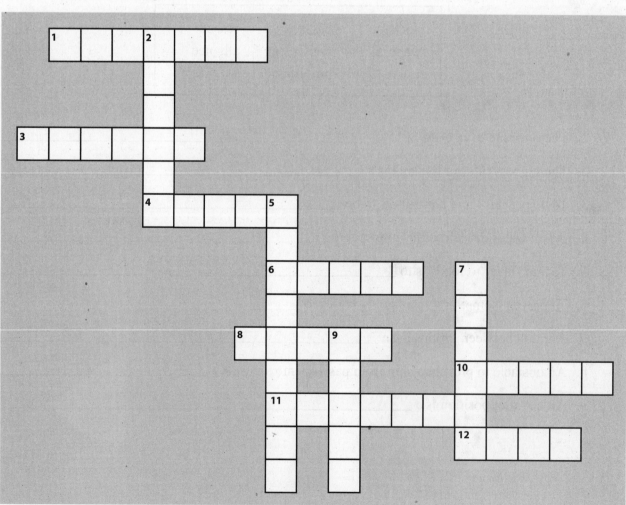

Name _____ Date _____

F A time line is a good way to put events in the correct order. It can also be used to organize some kinds of materials into a shorter, more readable form. To fill out a time line, you must understand dates. Look back at the selection titled "A Look at Salt and Spices" and the "Additional Information" boxes in Activity C. Find all the dates mentioned and place them on the time line below. Start with the earliest date at the top of the line and continue adding dates in order until the latest date is at the bottom end of the line. Add the information about what happened.

The History of Salt and Spices—Time Line

Selection 10

The Mystery of the Singing Bat

One day in December 1994, Barbara French began her daily routine. You might be surprised to learn what kind of routine she keeps. She takes care of Mexican free-tailed bats (*Tadarida brasiliensis*). The bats she cares for have been hurt and can't return to the wild. French thought this December day would be like any other, but it wasn't. She got a huge surprise. In fact, the surprise was the beginning of a scientific discovery.

As French was feeding the bats, she heard an unfamiliar, bird-like song. She stopped to listen. She heard all of the normal sounds. She recognized the buzz that Hannah made whenever she was defending her favorite roosting spot. Then French heard Wheatley's squeal, and she could tell that another bat had chased him away from the mealworm tray. French also heard the chirp Amy made whenever she wanted to be fed by hand. But French had never heard this new song before.

She decided to solve the mystery. Each time she heard the song, she would pop her head into the bat cage. As soon as her head was inside, the singing would stop. It took Barbara two weeks to identify the singing bat. The singer was Hank, an adult male. He seemed to be singing to a small group of females in his roosting pocket. A roosting pocket is a handmade fabric pouch, or bag, in the bats' cage.

In the weeks that followed, the male bats became unusually bold and ready to fight. They chased each other constantly. Free-tailed bats ordinarily like to roost together—that is, they like the company of other bats. So French thought this aggressive behavior was odd.

French grew worried. Her familiar little bat colony was suddenly very different. The bats had been happy with each other for the past year. Of course, they sometimes squabbled, pushed, shoved, and swatted at each other. However, these were normal bat behaviors. Plus, the bats always settled their differences quickly. They didn't hurt each other, and the bat that started a fight usually tried to end the fight. He or she would snuggle up with the other bats as if to say, "I'm sorry." The entire colony seemed to work together to keep the peace. However, Hank was different.

One day French watched Hank attack Joshua, another bat. Hank darted from his roosting pocket. He buzzed loudly and chased Joshua around the cage. French decided that Joshua had probably moved too near Hank's territory. Before she could stop him, Hank caught Joshua and snagged his ear. Hank's anger bothered French, but what followed really upset her. Moments after she had rescued Joshua, he squeezed out of her hand. Joshua zoomed off, making an excursion into Hank's territory. Joshua seemed ready to fight back.

74

Because she didn't understand the bats' new behaviors, French decided to seek help. She called Amanda Lollar, a licensed expert in the care of captive Mexican free-tailed bats. Lollar informed French that Hank was probably "singing to his women." Lollar also told French to watch for pups that would probably be born during the summer. French was surprised that the explanation was so simple. The bats she took care of had problems that made it impossible for them to live on their own in the wild. French hadn't thought the bats were strong enough to have healthy pups.

The problems weren't over. French and the other bats found Hank's behavior too hard to manage. Hank fought with other males all the time. He bit Joshua's ear again. He even tried to attack French as she fed a female.

She noticed something else new. Three females that had been roosting with Hank suddenly began eating more. They ate everything Barbara fed them and still wanted more.

Finally, Hank's singing stopped. The females left Hank and moved into Wheatley's roosting area. Eventually, Hank became himself again. The Hank problem was solved, but a Wheatley problem began. Wheatley began to guard the females that were expecting babies. Wheatley became as fierce as Hank had been.

In June, as French was feeding the bats, she saw a little, pink pup about the size of a walnut. Although the baby was very young, he was able to follow his mother around inside the roosting pocket. Twelve days later, French saw the birth of a second pup. This baby was born with his eyes open. He was able to lick his tiny wings clean within minutes after birth.

French learned a lot from her experience with her bats. So did scientists who study bats. She was able to give scientists information they had never had before. Hank's music wasn't a mystery anymore. Neither was Wheatley's protective behavior. Thanks to Barbara French and her bats, scientists now know much more about the mating behaviors of Mexican free-tailed bats.

Why make observations?

How do you think Barbara's observations contributed to scientific knowledge? Write a short paragraph on another sheet of paper, telling what other animal researchers might learn from her discoveries.

A **Circle the correct answer for each question.**

1. What did Barbara French hear that caught her attention?

   a. an unusual buzz

   b. a quiet chirp

   c. a bird-like song

   d. a loud squeal

2. What is a roosting pocket?

   a. a wooden perch

   b. a pouch on a female bat

   c. a cardboard box

   d. a handmade fabric pouch

3. Which of these **best** helps the reader understand what the word *captive* means in the seventh paragraph?

   a. *Thanks to French and her bats, scientists now know much more about the mating behaviors of Mexican free-tailed bats.*

   b. *The bats she took care of had problems that made it impossible for them to live on their own in the wild.*

   c. *In June, as French was feeding the bats, she saw a little, pink pup about the size of a walnut.*

   d. *Three females that had been roosting with Hank suddenly began eating more.*

4. Which of these details **best** helps the reader know what the author means in the last paragraph by "protective behavior"?

   a. When the three females left Hank's roosting area, they moved into Wheatley's roosting area.

   b. After Hank's singing stopped, Wheatley started causing problems for French.

   c. Bats sometimes chased Wheatley away from the tray of mealworms.

   d. Wheatley started guarding the female bats that were expecting babies.

5. Which of these describes the organization of the entire selection?

   a. Events are described in the order in which they happened.

   b. A problem and the eventual solution are described.

   c. Two types of bat colonies are compared and contrasted.

   d. The author states her opinions and provides support for each one.

6. Why did the author **most likely** write this selection?

   a. to describe the mating behaviors of Mexican free-tailed bats

   b. to describe a series of actions that led to increased knowledge about bats

   c. to explain the importance of observation when injured bats are cared for

   d. to tell a story about the interactions of Mexican free-tailed bats in a colony

B **Answer the questions on the lines provided.**

1. What did Barbara French realize after talking to Amanda Lollar?

_____

_____

2. What are two adjectives that describe French? Give support for your choices.

_____

_____

_____

C **Write a summary on the lines below of the selection titled "The Mystery of the Singing Bat." Remember that a summary is a brief restatement of the main points of a piece of writing.**

_____

_____

_____

_____

_____

_____

_____

_____

_____

_____

_____

_____

_____

_____

_____

_____

Name _____   Date _____

D Read the following selection about bats. In each paragraph, write *M* on the line before the sentence that contains the main idea. Before supporting details, write *SD*. Before slightly related facts, write *SR*.

Bats

1. _____ Bats sleep during the day and hunt for food at night. _____ They are nocturnal. _____ Most bats are insectivores, or eat insects. _____ Bats help keep the insect population under control. _____ One small bat can eat up to 600 mosquitoes, moths, or other insects in an hour. _____ In Texas, there are about 20 million bats living in Braken Cave. _____ They are Mexican free-tailed bats, and they eat about 200 tons of insects every night. _____ Some kinds of bats eat fish, frogs, birds, scorpions, and mice. _____ Some eat fruits and plants.

2. _____ There are also bats that eat pollen and nectar. _____ Nectar is a sweet liquid found inside a plant or flower. _____ Some bats have long noses that they can push down into the center of flowers to find nectar and pollen. _____ Bats are important because they are pollinators for many plants, including bananas. _____ Pollinators are animals that spread pollen. _____ Pollen is a dusty substance that fertilizes plants.

3. _____ Most fruit-eating bats cannot digest seeds in the fruit they eat. _____ The seeds leave the bats' bodies in the form of waste. _____ Waste is undigested food that leaves an animal's body in droppings. _____ Some of the seeds grow into new fruit trees.

4. _____ Bat waste is called guano. _____ Guano provides fertilizer for growing crops. _____ Many people around the world use guano to make the soil healthy and full of nutrients that are good for growing plants.

5. _____ There are almost 1,000 species of bats. _____ Bats are divided into two main groups called megabats and microbats. _____ Megabats are very large, and microbats are small. _____ Most bats fall into the microbats category. _____ Most microbats weigh less than 2 ounces (56.7 grams). _____ The smallest microbat is a bumblebee bat, which is found in Thailand. _____ It is the size of a fingernail and weighs less than a dime.

6. _____ There are nearly 200 species of megabats. _____ Flying foxes are the largest of all the megabats. _____ They can weigh up to 4 pounds (1.8 kg) and have wingspans up to 6 feet (1.8 m).

7. _____ Some bats have spots or other color patterns on their wings. _____ Colors, shapes, and patterns help the bats blend in with their habitat. _____ This is called camouflage. _____ Camouflage makes it difficult for the bat's enemies to see them. _____ Speckled bats can blend in with an environment that is made up of bark or rocks. _____ Red, orange, and gold bats can hide in fruit trees and look like ripe fruit.

8. _____ Bats have unusual features that set them apart from other animals. _____ One bat, the leaf-nosed bat, has a nose with flaps of skin that look like leaves. _____ Bats have tails of different lengths. _____ The tails of some bats are short. _____ Other bats have tails that stick out past their legs. _____ Some bats are tailless._____ The wings of bats are covered by a thin tissue of skin called a membrane. _____ Each wing has four long fingers and one thumb with a claw. _____ A bat's wings are attached to its hind legs, and the membrane stretches behind the legs.

9. _____ While hunting food at night, bats make a series of high-pitched sounds that are too high for people to hear. _____ When the sounds hit an object, they bounce back to the bat's ears. _____ This is also how an echo works. _____ Bats use the sounds to find and catch flying insects in the dark. _____ The ability to use echoes to locate objects is called echolocation.

© Houghton Mifflin Harcourt Publishing Company

Name _____   Date _____

E Choose a word from below to complete each sentence. Some words will not be used.

compete	roosting	nocturnal
squabble	pollinators	nectar
environment	echolocation	insectivores
territory	membrane	undigested
excursion	licensed	fertilizer

1. Animals that spread pollen are _____.

2. Bats resting on their perch or in their pouches are _____.

3. To struggle against another for something is to _____.

4. Bouncing sound off objects to locate them is called _____.

5. A very thin piece of skin is a _____.

6. Animals that are active at night are _____.

7. Bat guano that is used to improve soil is called _____.

8. A trip is an _____.

9. To have little arguments is to _____.

10. An animal's surroundings are its _____.

From the selection called "Bats" in Activity D, list four positive things that bats do for people and the environment. Use a word from the word list above in each of your four answers.

_____

_____

_____

_____

_____

_____

_____

F A hypothesis is a guess that is made to explain a certain event or fact until the actual cause can be proved. Scientists Barbara French and Amanda Lollar had a hypothesis about why Hank was "singing." They used their hypothesis, or guess, until they could prove what was true. Read each of the following paragraphs. Write a hypothesis to explain what you think is happening in each paragraph. Then write what you would do to prove your hypothesis.

1. Snow has covered the ground, and the temperature has been below freezing for days. However, this morning you awake to find puddles all over the sidewalk. The icicles along your roofline are dripping.

    Hypothesis: _____

    _____

    What could you do to prove your hypothesis? _____

    _____

    _____

2. You think you feel the floor shaking. Then, books on the shelves begin to fall over. Glasses in the kitchen cabinets are clinking. You notice the chandelier over the dining table is swinging. Pictures begin to fall off the walls.

    Hypothesis: _____

    _____

    What could you do to prove your hypothesis? _____

    _____

    _____

3. You and a friend go to a pond. You each find a frog to enter in the local frog-jumping race. When you bring the frogs back home, you let them out of their boxes. Your friend's frog hops away quickly. Your frog takes one slow hop and then quits.

    Hypothesis: _____

    _____

    What could you do to prove your hypothesis? _____

    _____

    _____

G Observation is a very important trait for scientists and learners of all kinds to develop. Look at the two graphics below, read the labels, and compare the structure of a human ear to a bat ear. Make a list of the likenesses you observe. Then make a list of the differences you observe.

Human Ear

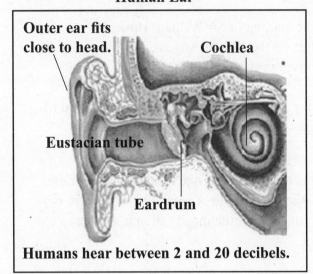

Outer ear fits close to head.

Cochlea

Eustacian tube

Eardrum

Humans hear between 2 and 20 decibels.

Bat Ear

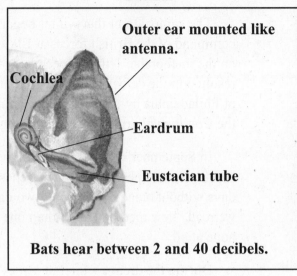

Outer ear mounted like antenna.

Cochlea

Eardrum

Eustacian tube

Bats hear between 2 and 40 decibels.

Likenesses

_____

_____

_____

_____

_____

Differences

_____

_____

_____

_____

_____

_____

Selection 11: Paired

Read this excerpt from *Washington at Valley Forge*. It describes the situation that General George Washington and his army had to endure while holding camp during the winter of 1777–1778.

The campaign of that winter began on the landing of Sir William Howe in command of the British forces at Elkton, Del., on the 18th of August, 1777, and closed on the memorable 11th of December of the same year in Whitemarsh, Penn., which resulted in the defeat of Washington at Brandywine and Germantown, the occupation of Philadelphia by the British army during the following winter, and the withdrawal of the Continental army to the uninviting heights of Valley Forge.

In September, 1777, Washington wrote: "At least one thousand men were barefooted and performed the marches in that condition." At one time they were three days without bread; on another, two days without a particle of meat. Of still a third day we read, "few men had more than one shirt, many only the moiety of one, and more none at all."

During the dreary winter at Valley Forge, Washington wrote (February 16, 1778): "For some days past there has been little less than a famine in the camp. A part of the army has been a week without any kind of flesh, and the rest three or four days. Naked and starving as they are we cannot enough admire the incomparable patience and fidelity of the soldiers that they have not been ere this excited by their sufferings to a general mutiny and dispersion."

At no period of the war, wrote Chief Justice Marshall, "had the American army been reduced to a situation of greater peril than during the winter at Valley Forge. More than once they were absolutely without food. Even while their condition was less desperate in this respect, their stock of provisions was so scanty that there was seldom at any time in the stores a quantity sufficient for the use of the troops for a week. Consequently, had the enemy moved out in force, the American army could not have continued in camp. The want of provisions would have forced them out of it, and their deplorable condition with respect to clothes disabled them from **keeping the field**[1] in winter. The returns on the first of February exhibit the astonishing number of 3,989 men in camp unfit for duty for want of clothes. Of this number, scarcely a man had a pair of shoes. Even among those returned as capable of duty very many were so badly clad that exposure to the colds of the season must have destroyed them." Out of 17,000 men occupying Valley Forge, no more than 5,012 could be considered as effective **rank and file**.[2]

---

[1] holding their position in the face of opposition
[2] common soldiers, not including officers

"Yet, amidst all this suffering, day after day," remarks Lossing, "surrounded by frost and snow, patriotism was still warm and hopeful in the hearts of the soldiers, and the love of self was merged in the holy sentiment of love of country. It was one of the most trying scenes in the life of Washington; but a cloud of doubt seldom darkened the serene atmosphere of his hopes. He knew that the cause was just and holy, and his faith and confidence in God as a defender and helper of right were as steady in the ministrations of vigor to his soul as were the pulsations of his heart to his limbs. In perfect reliance upon Divine Providence he moved in the midst of crushed hopes, and planned brilliant schemes for the future."

Dr. Waldo, an army surgeon who served at Valley Forge during the dreadful winter of 1777–78, has left a diary of the events of that time, in which he wrote: "The winter passed in Valley Forge was the gloomiest period of the war. The men were encamped in cold, comfortless huts, with little food or clothing. Barefooted they left on the ground their tracks in blood. Few had blankets, and straw could not be obtained."

Dr. Albigence Waldo was of French descent, . . . and died January 20, 1794, the result of his sufferings at Valley Forge. His diary at Valley Forge begins on November 10, 1777, and his entry for that day ends with "No salt to eat dinner with." . . . After sickness and much personal suffering Dr. Waldo, on December 18th, wrote: "Universal thanksgiving—a roasted pig at night! The army are poorly supplied with provisions, owing, it is said, to the neglect of the Commissary of Purchases. . . ."

It must now be apparent to the reader that the difficulties which beset Washington at that period whereof we write were of no common character, but, notwithstanding their intense sufferings, he had the rank and file of the troops with him. The spirit that animated the army when it lay encamped at Valley Forge in the memorable winter of 1777–78 was the love of country; it was not fighting for the spoils of conquest or the oppression of a race, but for a home. Harassed by tiresome marches and perpetual alarms, their life was one continual scene of hardship and danger; their feet were naked and bleeding amidst the driving snows of winter, and they lay down in that dreary camp to become acquainted with hunger, cold, and watchfulness. "The history of the world presents no parallel to the sublime heroism which, animated and sustained by the immortal Washington, upheld and sustained the cause of freedom through the glorious period of American history. What devotion and courage, and, alas, too what pity at the recital of their sufferings! Far from home, their sufferings unrelieved by their almost despairing country, no wife nor mother near to relieve their wants or close their eyes in death, they sank into the grave almost unnoticed, with no friendly tear but those of sorrowing comrades shed for their sufferings or mingled with their dust. The sufferings of the men at Valley Forge have consecrated the spot in every patriot heart; and while history, tradition, and art shall transmit the tragic story to remotest posterity as a sublime incentive to emulation when the impaired liberties of their country shall summon them to arms, just so long will their record be one that the ancient warriors of Greece or Rome might have envied."

What nobler tribute can be imagined that is contained in these words!

Name _____ Date _____

 A Choose a word that matches each definition or clue. Some words will not be used. Use a dictionary.

clad	capable	deplorable
peril	scanty	mingle
oppression	animated	sentiment
perpetual	consecrated	sublime

1. danger   _____

2. cruel or unjust treatment   _____

3. too small in amount; insufficient   _____

4. of such excellence that it inspires admiration   _____

5. never stopping or ending   _____

6. emotion or feeling   _____

7. causing grief, shock, or regret   _____

8. to have made sacred   _____

9. clothed   _____

10. to mix   _____

B The following words from the selection have more than one meaning. Use a dictionary to help you determine which meaning is used in the selection. Write that meaning in your own words on the line. (*Hint:* All the words are nouns.) The first one is done for you.

1. stores   *supplies of things kept to be used in the future*

2. stock   _____

3. spoils   _____

4. race   _____

5. recital   _____

6. character   _____

86

Selection 11: Paired
Core Skills Reading Comprehension, Grade 7

Name _____ Date _____

C **Circle the correct answer for each question.**

1. During the time period described in the selection, Washington's troops at Valley Forge suffered from all of the following *except*

   a. enemy attacks.

   b. lack of clothing.

   c. hunger.

   d. extreme cold.

2. Based on the selection, what is the *most likely* reason that only 5,012 of the 17,000 troops at Valley Forge could be "considered as effective rank and file"?

   a. The others could not have survived the cold while fighting due to a lack of proper clothes.

   b. The others had lost faith in General Washington after experiencing so much hardship.

   c. The others had died from battle, sickness, starvation, and exposure to the cold.

   d. The others would not have had sufficient energy to fight against enemy troops.

3. In paragraph five of the selection, personification is used to describe

   a. duty.

   b. history.

   c. patriotism.

   d. suffering.

4. Lossing uses figurative language in the fifth paragraph to contrast

   a. the sense of self-preservation with the devotion to General Washington.

   b. the love of self with the love of food and clothing.

   c. the soldiers' hearts with their freezing feet.

   d. the cold of the environment with the warmth of patriotism.

D **Read the following sentence from the selection.**

It must now be apparent to the reader that the difficulties which beset Washington at that period whereof we write were of no common character, but, notwithstanding their intense sufferings, he had the rank and file of the troops with him.

Briefly name evidence from the selection for each of the following ideas in this sentence.

1. Washington was troubled by difficulties at that period.

_____

_____

_____

2. The difficulties were of no common character.

_____

_____

_____

_____

3. The soldiers suffered intensely.

_____

_____

_____

_____

4. Washington had the support of the common soldiers.

_____

_____

_____

_____

Selection 12: Paired

The Letter

Sarah looked out the window at the bleak, snowy day. She refolded the worn letter that she and her parents had read so many times since it had arrived. It was the only letter they had received from her brother James since he had joined General Washington's army months before. Now they finally had proof that he was alive. Yet his words gave little comfort.

James's letter described life at Valley Forge. The weather was deadly cold, and there was little food. James told of long marches across the frozen ground. His shoes had long since fallen to pieces. He had walked many miles with only strips of leather tied around his feet. Many soldiers were barefoot and had no coat or blankets to keep them warm. Some had died of starvation and exposure to the cold.

Tears filled Sarah's eyes as she imagined her strong, happy brother suffering so much. How she would love to see him wrapped in a blanket in his chair by the fireplace! She thought about the many nights they had spent talking in front of the fire. She hoped with every fiber of her being that one evening they would repeat this simple act.

As terrible as his situation was, James wrote that he would support General Washington to the end. He believed in the Revolution. The British laws seemed to strangle the rights of free Americans. He was sure the colonies would one day be free of British rule. He wanted Americans to have freedom of speech and a better quality of life. All of his suffering would be well worth it if his country could be a better place to live in.

Sarah laid the letter on the table and returned to her chair by the fire. Her mother looked up from the quilt she was stitching and gave Sarah an understanding smile.

Sarah picked up the scarf she was knitting and began to work her needles with a quick steady rhythm. Long after her parents went to bed, Sarah continued to work. Each time her fingers grew tired, she looked over to the letter on the table. Then the soft clicking of her needles would begin again.

After reading James's letter, Sarah's father had sworn he would deliver supplies to the troops no matter how difficult the trip might be. As Sarah knitted, she thought about what she could do to help the soldiers. She decided she would try to get as much support as she could from the people in her town.

Sarah was delighted to see how responsive the townspeople were. The women gathered odd bits of fabric to use in making quilts. Young girls pieced together bits of yarn to make scarves, hats, and gloves. Some people donated warm clothing and blankets. Others donated preserved and fresh foods. A few people gave up their own precious shoes when they heard about the soldiers' desperate need for them. Most importantly, people sent letters to the soldiers expressing their appreciation for supporting their new country.

Sarah's family couldn't believe what a wonderful town they lived in! Everyone had turned out to be so supportive of the soldiers and had done whatever they could to help.

Sarah's father, along with several other people, delivered the supplies to the troops in wagons. Among them were the many scarves that Sarah had knitted during the long winter nights.

After a difficult journey back home, her father arrived with letters from a few of the soldiers expressing their gratitude. As Sarah read the first one, tears sprang to her eyes. Her father quietly told her that the same thing had happened to many of the soldiers when they saw the supplies.

A Circle the correct answer for each question.

1. How does Sarah feel about her brother?
   a. She resents his leaving the family to go fight.
   b. She is disappointed that he supports General Washington.
   c. She is worried about him and wants to help him.
   d. She is confused and does not understand his suffering.

2. Why is the fourth paragraph important to the selection?
   a. It explains the reason James left his family to fight in the army.
   b. It gives information about the type of leader Washington was.
   c. It describes the trouble James had in the past with the British.
   d. It describes the hopes of all Americans to have a better country.

3. What is the theme of this selection?

    a. writing letters during a war

    b. making sacrifices for a greater cause

    c. supporting leaders during a war

    d. keeping in touch with one's family

4. Which of the following is *most* important to the problem in the selection?

    a. the fireplace   **c.** the surrounding countryside

    b. the colonial family's home   **d.** winter at Valley Forge

5. Who is telling this selection?

    a. Sarah   **c.** James

    b. Sarah's mother   **d.** someone other than a character

6. This selection is an example of

    a. a historical fiction.   **c.** a historical essay.

    b. a biography.   **d.** an autobiography.

B   Answer the questions on the lines provided.

1. Read this sentence from the fourth paragraph.

> **The British laws seemed to strangle the rights of free Americans.**

    Explain the impact of the word *strangle*.

    _____

    _____

    _____

2. Read these sentences from the fifth paragraph.

> **Each time her fingers grew tired, she looked over to the letter on the table. Then the soft clicking of her needles would begin again.**

    What does the author accomplish with these sentences?

    _____

    _____

3. Describe the contrast between the tears Sarah sheds in the third paragraph and the tears she sheds in the last paragraph.

_____

_____

_____

C **Writers can make characters come alive by using dialogue—that is, by having characters talk to each other. In addition, the writer can give the reader even more clues about a character by using direct internal dialogue—that is, by revealing a character's direct thoughts.**

1. In the example below, underline the direct internal dialogue.

Sarah laid James's letter on the table and looked at her mother. "He's so young to be in such a horrid situation," she said.

Her mother said, "You're quite right. As his mother, my heart is weeping." She sighed. "And yet, as an American, my heart is swollen with pride for him."

After her mother had gone to bed, Sarah thought, "I can't be there besides James. But there must be *something* I can do to contribute toward the cause he's willing to die for."

2. Read the last paragraph of the selection. Then write a dialogue that might have taken place between Sarah and her father, based on the content of this paragraph. Include at least one instance of direct internal dialogue.

_____

_____

_____

_____

_____

_____

_____

_____

D **Think about the excerpt from *Washington at Valley Forge* and "The Letter." Answer the questions on the lines provided.**

1. Which selection gives the reader more background information on why the Americans were fighting against the British?

_____

2. Which part of the excerpt from *Washington at Valley Forge* is contradicted by the events in "The Letter"? Explain your answer.

_____

_____

3. How closely does the description in the excerpt from *Washington at Valley Forge* of the soldiers' suffering match the description of this in "The Letter"? Explain your answer.

_____

_____

_____

4. Compare the author's ***most likely*** purpose for writing *Washington at Valley Forge* with the author's ***most likely*** purpose for writing "The Letter."

_____

_____

_____

_____

5. The *tone* of a text is the attitude the writer takes toward a character, toward the audience, or toward the subject of the work. Compare and contrast the tone of the excerpt from *Washington at Valley Forge* with the tone of "The Letter." Explain your choice of words to describe the tone of each selection.

_____

_____

_____

_____

_____

6. Which of the two selections did you enjoy reading more? Why?

_____

_____

_____

93

Name _____ Date _____

 Read this excerpt of a poem written by a man who fought against the British during the Revolutionary War. Then answer the questions on the lines provided.

On taking a retrospective view of my suffering while in the Revolutionary army, in which I served three years and a half, in which time I suffered with hunger, cold, and want of clothing.

> On the cold earth I oft[1] have lain
> Oppress'd with hunger, toil, and pain
> While storms and tempests roar'd around
> And frost and snow had cloth'd the ground
> The British troops, did us assail[2],
> In storms of snow, and rattling hail.
> All this with patience long we bore[3]
> Until that sanguine[4] war was o'er, . . .

[1] often
[2] attack
[3] endured
[4] bloody

1. What is the rhyme scheme in the poem?

   _____

   _____

2. Look at the last line of the excerpt. How did the author make the word *over* rhyme with *bore*?

   _____

   _____

3. Read the excerpt aloud. Notice the regular rhythm of the stressed and unstressed syllables—that is, words or parts of words that you say more loudly or more quietly. How do the rhyme scheme and the regular rhythm emphasize the suffering that the man endured during the war?

   _____

   _____

   _____

   _____

Selection 13

121 Sparrow Lane
Mason City, Iowa
November 12, 2014

Carlos Gonzales
P.O. Box 122
Des Moines, Iowa

Dear Carlos,

Everyone here is fine and looking forward to the Thanksgiving holiday. My classes have been so hard this semester that I can't wait for the break. Even Mom and Dad seem more eager than usual for the holiday to get here. I just wish you were going to be here to share it with us.

Mom said that you called Thursday night while I was at a rehearsal for the school play. Did I tell you that I got the lead role? I'm spending every spare minute memorizing my lines. Anyway, I'm sorry that I didn't get to talk to you. Maybe I could have convinced you to come home for Thanksgiving. Mom said you're going home with your roommate. Where is Durango, Colorado, anyway?

Everyone will be here—Abuelita, Abuelito, Uncle Eduardo, Aunt Anna, Michael, Mom, Dad, and of course, me. Well, I guess not everyone since you'll be who knows how many miles away. I don't know if you've thought much about Abuelito lately. He's getting old, you know. Mom said that the last time Aunt Anna visited, Abuelito couldn't remember her name. I bet he'd remember you, though. Abuelito always really loved you. Thanksgiving would be a perfect time to see him. Don't you agree?

It's been a while since we've talked. Since you went away to college, I haven't had anyone to talk to about those really personal things. You know what I mean. I don't want you to worry or anything. I don't have any major, horrible problem right now. But you never know when one's going to come up, and then what will I do? We've never talked about how to handle personal emergencies while you're away. It seems like Thanksgiving would be a perfect time to talk about that.

I just thought of another reason you should come home for Thanksgiving. How can we have our traditional family game if you aren't here? We don't have enough players without you. Do you remember last year when I made that extra point just seconds before we were called into dinner? I think that was the best Thanksgiving game we've ever had, don't you? I wonder. Does your roommate's family play football on Thanksgiving? I hope you'll tell him how much fun we all have at our house playing together. Tell him if he joins us, we'll take it easy on him! Does your roommate know that you led your high school team to the district playoffs last year? Here's a drawing of you.

I think I've almost run out of things to say. Wait. There's something else. Mrs. Sánchez came by the other day. I heard her tell Mom that Marcie was coming home for Thanksgiving. I haven't seen Marcie since you and she took me camping right before school started. Remember how beautiful the stars were? And it was so much fun telling spooky stories around the fire. That was a great time. Just thinking about it makes me want to go camping again. I wonder if Marcie would like to put up a tent with us in the backyard. She and I could have our own Thanksgiving dinner out there. Of course, camping might not be as much fun if it's just the two of us. It wouldn't feel right without you.

Well, Carlos, I think I'm at the end of this letter. I don't know what else to write. I'd like to see you at Thanksgiving. It won't be the same if you're not here. Of course, I'm not trying to pressure you. It's your decision. I know you'll do the right thing. Besides, you're probably not as crazy about Abuelita's famous homemade cranberry sauce as I am. And I can't remember if lemon icebox pie is still your favorite dessert. I'm making one, you know. There's going to be a lot of really good food. Turkey and a special salsa dressing, Mama's special spicy beans, Tia's sweet potatoes, and much, much more. Oh, well. I bet the food in Durango is pretty good, too. I really am going to say goodbye now. I sure miss you. I will be thinking about you over the holiday. I hope you have a great Thanksgiving. I'll do the best I can without you.

Your best and only sister,

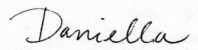

Daniella

P.S. Does your roommate like lemon icebox pie? I can make a pumpkin pie if he likes that better.

A **Circle the correct answer for each question.**

1. What is Daniella's *main* purpose for writing the letter?

   a. She wants Carlos to go camping with their friend Marcie and her.

   b. She wants Carlos to come home for the holiday.

   c. She wants to tell Carlos how much she cares for him.

   d. She wants to meet Carlos's college roommate.

2. Why does Daniella ask questions about Carlos's roommate's likes and dislikes?

   a. She has a crush on the roommate.

   b. She is showing polite interest in the roommate's feelings.

   c. She hopes to hide her dislike for the roommate by asking about him.

   d. She hopes to interest the roommate in joining them for the holiday.

3. What are two arguments Daniella uses to achieve her goal with Carlos?

   a. Abuelito's age; the family football game

   b. a personal problem; the bad food in Durango, Colorado

   c. Abuelito's love for Carlos; the illness of their aunt Anna

   d. delicious pumpkin pie; the possibility of camping with Marcie

4. Which paragraph from the letter provides the *best* evidence of what Carlos and Daniella's relationship is like?

   a. fourth paragraph   c. sixth paragraph

   b. fifth paragraph   d. seventh paragraph

5. Which word best describes the tone of Daniella's letter?

   a. *angry*   c. *coaxing*

   b. *disappointed*   d. *pouting*

B **Answer the questions on the lines provided.**

1. How does Daniella's closing about being his "only sister" reinforce her purpose?

   _____

   _____

2. How does the letter let the reader know how Daniella feels about her brother?

   _____

   _____

   _____

C Daniella's letter was sent through the post office. This way of communicating has come to be called "snail mail" because of how slow it is compared to electronic communication—that is, communicating through texting, sending emails, or posting to a website. Read the following short piece to learn about the rules you should use when posting. Then answer the questions below.

Rules showing the polite way to behave are called "etiquette." If you don't use good etiquette, you might not get invited again to someone's house. Rules showing the polite way to behave on the Internet (or "net" for short) are called "netiquette." If you ignore netiquette, you might get banned from ever posting anything again on a website.

Many online services and websites have their own netiquette—guidelines or rules—that have to be followed by everyone who posts something. And the posts are monitored! So anyone who disregards the rules may be blocked from posting in the future. This is why it's important to familiarize yourself with the netiquette of the website you'd like to post to.

Here are some general netiquette tips.

- Avoid using all caps. TYPING IN CAPS is the equivalent of shouting. So hold your voice down and keep your finger off the "Caps Lock" key. Also, one exclamation point usually does the trick.

- Don't include personal attacks, hurtful language, or bad words. When you're online, you feel anonymous, and you may be tempted to use language you wouldn't use in person. But resist that temptation if you want to continue posting to the website.

- Stay on topic and say something meaningful—not just "cool" or "LOL." And don't use your post to promote your ideas about something or someone else.

- So that the greatest number of website visitors can understand your post, use correct spelling and grammar. Also, avoid slang unless you're sure that everyone will understand the word or phrase.

1. What does *netiquette* mean?

   _____

2. What might happen if you don't follow the netiquette of a website you want to post to?

   _____

3. Why should you use capital letters sparingly in a post?

   _____

4. Since you can't easily be identified on a website, what might you be tempted to do?

   _____

5. Why should you avoid using slang in a post?

   _____

D **Some words have more than one meaning and pronunciation. Study the word below and its meanings. Then write the letter of the correct meaning of the word next to each sentence.**

reject: a. (rē´jĕct) *n*: something that cannot be used due to damage or some other reason

b. (rĕ jĕct´) *v*: to refuse to accept, consider, hear, or use

The vase is a *reject* because it is cracked.

The judge will *reject* the vote results if they are not submitted on time.

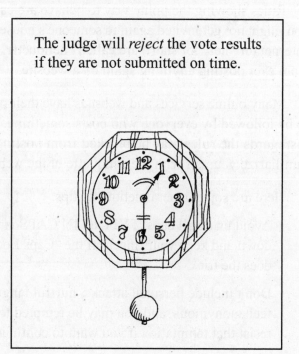

_____ 1. They *reject* the idea because they do not agree with it.

_____ 2. Sam's clay pot was a *reject* because it had a chip.

_____ 3. Laneesha *rejected* her sister's arguments because they were slanted.

_____ 4. The factory line came to a stop as the *reject*, a flawed toy, was removed.

_____ 5. The shoes were scuffed and heelless, *rejects* to be thrown on the garbage pile.

_____ 6. Damian is a poor sport and *rejects* any offer of apology.

_____ 7. Rolando was sure that the story he'd submitted for the contest would be a *reject*.

_____ 8. Mr. Yakamoto expects his supervisor to *reject* his proposal.

Selection 14

A Historic Victory

In Spanish, the name *Cinco de Mayo* means the 5th of May. It is a Mexican holiday that all Americans should observe. The holiday celebrates a historic victory in the city of Puebla, Mexico, on May 5, 1862. Two groups of soldiers fought each other. A small Mexican army of soldiers and ordinary citizens battled against French forces. The French forces had better equipment and training, but the Mexican army won the battle.

The Mexican army's victory was minor. It did not end French control of Mexico. In fact, the French would conquer Mexico and rule over it for five more years. However, the Battle of Puebla was significant. It showed that ordinary Mexican citizens could fight against a powerful foreign force and win.

Why were French forces in Mexico? When the Battle of Puebla happened, Mexico was in financial trouble. The Mexican-American War had ended in 1848, and Mexico owed other countries a substantial amount of money—debts it had accumulated to help pay the costs of the war. The national treasury was almost empty. So in 1861, Mexican President Benito Juárez said that Mexico would not pay what it owed for two years. Despite the President's promise to pay off the debt, France, Spain, and Great Britain did not want to wait. Each country sent a military force to collect the money Mexico owed them. Later, the British and Spanish realized that Napoleon III, ruler of France, intended to take over Mexico. The British and Spanish worked out an agreement with President Juárez and then withdrew. The French troops stayed.

The French military feared no one. They had not lost a single battle in 50 years. The French thought the Mexicans would give up without a fight. They were mistaken.

Texas-born General Ignacio Zaragoza waited for the French forces to come. He was ordered to defend President Juárez and the city of Puebla. The general commanded about 4,000 troops, which included farmers whose weapons were old rifles and farm tools.

Six thousand French soldiers charged the city. After only two hours, the battle ended. Many French soldiers had been killed or wounded. Despite the odds against them, the Mexican army had defeated what was perhaps the most powerful army in the world. This victory on May 5, 1862, strengthened the pride of the Mexican people and brought them together. It gave them determination to expulse the French from their land—even after Maximillian, Archduke of Austria, arrived in 1864 when Napoleon invited him to be Emperor of Mexico.

The victory at the Battle of Puebla was also important for Americans. After the French were defeated, President Juárez went to northern Mexico. There, he set up a temporary but powerful government to fight the French. The government's position in northern Mexico prevented the French army from getting supplies to southern Confederate rebels during the American Civil War. Due to these events in Mexico, the northern Union army in the United States had another year to grow stronger. In July 1863, little more than one year after the Battle of Puebla, the Union forces defeated the Confederates at the Battle of Gettysburg.

After the Civil War, Generals Philip Sheridan and Ulysses S. Grant went to the border between Texas and Mexico. The generals gave Mexican troops the supplies they needed to combat the French. By 1867, Napoleon had withdrawn all French troops from Mexico. The brave Mexican people controlled their country again.

Cinco de Mayo is not a celebration of Mexico's independence. It marks a day when Mexicans discovered how strong and determined they were. Cinco de Mayo is a celebration of national pride. Today, many Mexican-Americans have parades and festivals on Cinco de Mayo. They play traditional music and dance. They share traditional food, arts, and crafts.

Some historians think that the United States should celebrate Cinco de Mayo. If President Juárez's government in northern Mexico had not prevented the French from getting supplies to the Confederate army, the American Civil War might have ended differently. If the Confederates had won the war, the United States might now be two countries instead of one. This in itself is sufficient reason for U.S. citizens to celebrate Cinco de Mayo. Yet there is even another good reason. By recognizing Cinco de Mayo, U.S. citizens could learn more about people who showed great valor. They could perhaps better appreciate what they owe those few, brave Mexican soldiers and ordinary citizens who fought in Puebla in 1862.

Which holiday?

Holidays are important to different people for different reasons. What holiday is important in your family? Why? Write a brief explanation on another sheet of paper.

A **Circle the correct answer for each question.**

1. This selection is a

    a. compare and contrast article.   **c.** short mystery.

    b. biographical essay.   **d.** work of historical nonfiction.

2. What does Cinco de Mayo celebrate?

    a. Mexico's contribution toward the Union forces winning the American Civil War

    b. the Mexican victory over the British and Spanish in the city of Puebla

    c. the Mexican people's success in forcing the French out of their country

    d. the Mexican victory over the French in the city of Puebla

3. What was an indirect result of the Battle of Puebla?

    a. Southern Confederate troops could not get supplies from the French in Mexico.

    b. Mexican troops later were unable to attack the United States.

    c. British, French, and Spanish troops later were unable to attack the United States.

    d. Northern Union troops could not get supplies from the French in Mexico.

4. Cinco de Mayo marks a day that Mexicans discovered

    a. how weak the French were.   **c.** that they could help the United States.

    b. how strong they were.   **d.** that the Spanish and British were their allies.

5. Which word *best* describes the tone of this selection?

    a. personal   **b.** concerned   **c.** formal   **d.** sympathetic

6. Which of these sentences from the last two paragraphs is a statement of opinion?

    a. *Some historians think all Americans should celebrate Cinco de Mayo.*

    b. *Cinco de Mayo is a celebration of national pride.*

    c. *Today, many Mexican-Americans have parades and festivals on Cinco de Mayo.*

    d. *This in itself is sufficient reason for all Americans to celebrate Cinco de Mayo.*

B **Answer the questions on the lines provided.**

1. Explain why the Mexican victory over the French forces was surprising.

    _____

    _____

2. Explain the importance of the third and fourth paragraphs.

    _____

    _____

3. Explain how money was an indirect factor in the Battle of Puebla.

_____

_____

_____

4. What is the author's point of view about Cinco de Mayo? Give support for your answer.

_____

_____

_____

_____

C **Choose a word to complete each sentence.**

historic	accumulated	significant
superior	expulse	valor
temporary	financial	commanded

1. The soldiers demonstrated their _____ by holding off the enemy for five days.

2. The raising of the U.S. flag on the moon was an _____ occasion.

3. The headquarters of the company is in a _____ location; its permanent location will be in Cleveland, Ohio.

4. Despite great efforts, the people were unable to _____ the enemy forces from their country.

5. The nation is currently experiencing great _____ difficulties and will be unable to pay back its loans from other nations.

6. The outcome of the election is of _____ interest to Dr. Holtzman, professor of political science.

7. The captain _____ his soldiers to prepare for battle.

8. Due to the scientists involved, the country's space program is _____ to that of any other country.

9. Positive comments about the new website have _____ rapidly over the past few weeks.

D **Read the list carefully. Then follow the directions.**

Possible Experts

the head of the Hispanic Studies department of the local college

the researcher at the local natural history museum

a neighbor who is interested in Mexican pottery

your history teacher at school

a friend who is taking Spanish

the head librarian at the local city library

the director of the Mexican culture section of the local art museum

---

1. Name the four experts you think would help you the *most* in finding out more about the history of Cinco de Mayo. List them in order, beginning with most knowledgeable.

   a. _____

   _____

   b. _____

   _____

   c. _____

   _____

   d. _____

2. What questions would you ask the experts?

   _____

   _____

   _____

   _____

   _____

   _____

   _____

The experts you picked have listened to your questions. They have made suggestions about research topics.

The experts suggested you look for the following:

- The history of Mexico and the city of Puebla
- Key people involved in the Battle of Puebla and in politics at the time
- The Civil War
- French history around 1862
- Hispanic culture and festivals

You then go to the encyclopedia to look up information about the topics the experts mentioned. In which volumes should you look?

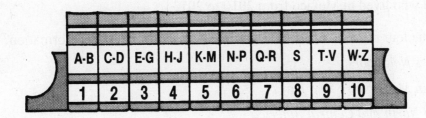

Think of at least eight specific topics you can look up. Write the information on the lines below. Use the column headings given.

	Volume	Letters	Topic
1.	_____	_____	_____
2.	_____	_____	_____
3.	_____	_____	_____
4.	_____	_____	_____
5.	_____	_____	_____
6.	_____	_____	_____
7.	_____	_____	_____
8.	_____	_____	_____

Name _____ Date _____

F Lisette and Yoli Garza are going to spend a month traveling in Mexico. To plan their trip carefully, they will look up as much information as possible and speak to people who can help them. Circle the answers to the questions below.

1. What are the five *best* sources of relevant information about their trip?

   a. a librarian

   b. a guard in a museum

   c. a Mexican artist

   d. a clerk at the airline office

   e. a travel agent

   f. an Internet website sponsored by the Mexican government

   g. a friend who lived in Mexico from 2010 to 2013

2. What are the four references that will give them the *most* relevant information?

   a. *Mexico's Neighbors*

   b. *Travel in Mexico on $50 a Day*

   c. *Atlas of North and Central America*

   d. *Recipes from Mexico*

   e. bus schedule of trips around Mexico

   f. *Travel to South America on $50 a Day*

   g. *Ancient Mexican Sights*

3. All these people have written books. Which three authors would *most likely* give the Garza sisters relevant information?

   a. Jimmy Grant, a mechanic in South Texas, who services planes from Mexico

   b. Marta Salas, the publicity agent of the Mexican Tourist Center

   c. Enrique Palmas, who wrote *Life of a Mexican Butterfly*

   d. Elena Valles, a writer who travels all over the world and reviews airplanes, hotels, and restaurants

   e. Sarah Goldberg, a geography professor, who writes for travel magazines

Skills Review: Selections 8–14

(A) **Read the selection below. The author is trying to convince you to take a speech class. Underline the main persuasive argument(s) in each paragraph. Then answer the questions that follow.**

Take a Speech Class!

1   What happened the last time you stood up to speak to your class? Did your knees shake? Did your voice wobble? Did your eyes blink in rapid motion? Did sweat roll from under your arms down your sides? If your answer to any of these important questions is yes, then you should take a speech class.

2   There are so many good reasons for taking a speech class that it's hard to decide where to begin. But I'll try anyway. Taking a speech class makes you confident. What does it mean to be confident? For one thing, it means you can stand up to talk without shaking like the last leaf on a tree in a heavy windstorm. It means you can speak in a language that sounds like English. It also means your classmates won't roll their eyes while you're talking. They'll be listening. And they'll listen because you sound like you know what you're talking about.

3   So, how do you make this happen? In a speech class, you'll learn to think before you speak. No doubt, you've heard that one before. But in this case, it's good advice. Here's why. You can't talk effectively about something you don't know anything about. People can tell when the person who's talking to them doesn't know what he or she is talking about. They can also tell when someone isn't prepared to speak. You've probably noticed that yourself. How long does a speaker like that keep your attention? Not long.

4   Thinking before speaking can make you confident, and this is what you'll practice in a speech class. Let's say, for example, that on the first day of school, your teacher gives you a homework assignment. You must come to school the next day ready to tell the class how you spent your summer vacation.

5   The night before class, you could decide to "wing it." Basically, that means you don't think about the assignment at all. You think the most important thing you can do to prepare is to show up for class. Well, we know what happens when you do that. Speech class will teach you how to prepare and rehearse a speech.

6 This time, sit down and make a list of everything you did over the summer. If the only thing on your list is "summer school," you have a problem. Your speech could be a disaster unless you add a little spice. I don't mean lie. I mean think harder! Speech class will help you learn about adding zip and spice by having you ask yourself questions. What happened in summer school? Whom did you meet? What special projects did you do? Whom did you sit with at lunchtime? Name two things you did that were outstanding. Do you understand where I'm going here?

7 Okay. Now that your list covers both sides of your paper, you're ready. Choose one or two things you really want to talk about. Learning about what not to talk about is just as important as learning what you *should* talk about. You'll learn this with practice in class.

8 Now, on a new piece of paper, write details about the one or two things you chose. But don't write every detail. Speech class teaches that relating a few main ideas well will capture your audience's attention. Go for the main ideas. List them in the order you want to talk about them. Then use a few words or phrases that will help you remember what you want to say about each main idea. When you reach the end, go stand in front of a mirror. Look yourself straight in the eye and start talking! Say everything you want to say to the class, and say it over and over again. Say it so often that you can remember what you want to say without using the piece of paper in your hands.

9 The big moment comes. It's your turn to talk. You've practiced your speech. You know what you want to say. The problem is that the people out there don't look like the person you saw in the mirror. But they are. They're just like you, only less prepared. Breathe deeply. Look at the crowd. Be brave. Move forward. This probably won't be the best speech you'll ever give, but it's a start. And after you finish speech class, no one will ever see your knees shaking again.

1. What does the author say you will do in a speech class that will make you confident?

a. listen to others who are prepared   **c.** make a list of possible topics

b. stand up to talk without shaking   **d.** think before speaking

2. Read this claim from the selection.

> **Learning about what not to talk about is just as important as learning about what you *should* talk about.**

Which paragraph provides the *best* support for this claim?

a. paragraph 6   **c.** paragraph 8

b. paragraph 7   **d.** paragraph 9

B Read the situation and the information about Joseph that follows. Then write a brief dialogue that fits the situation and provides clues about Joseph.

Joseph has recently moved to a new middle school. Although he wasn't shy at his old school, he feels painfully shy now. One day, he finally gets up the courage to start a conversation with Aiden, a guy in his math class who often makes people laugh.

_____

_____

_____

_____

_____

_____

_____

_____

_____

_____

_____

C Circle the word that completes the analogy.

1. *Work* is to *play* as *uncover* is to _____.

   work   bury   shovel

2. *Iris* is to *eye* as *finger* is to _____.

   ring   palm   hand

3. *Scream* is to *pain* as *laugh* is to _____.

   joke   laughter   giggle

4. *Spoon* is to *eat* as *telescope* is to _____.

   planets   observe   scientist

D Study the meanings of the word *stew*. Then write the letter of the correct meaning of the word next to each sentence.

> **stew:** a. *n*: a slowly cooked dish of meat and vegetables
> b. *n*: a state of great anxiety
> c. *v*: to cook slowly in a liquid in a closed dish
> d. *v*: to be in a state of worry or anxiety

_____ **1.** Walt has worked himself into a *stew* because he's afraid he'll be late.

_____ **2.** Aunt Luisa made a delicious *stew* for dinner last night.

_____ **3.** Miles is in his room *stewing* over the game his team lost.

_____ **4.** The tomatoes need to *stew* for at least 20 minutes.

_____ **5.** Are you going to stand there and *stew*, or do you want to help me clean up this mess?

E Circle the two synonyms in each group of words below.

1. emptied	irrigated	irritated	watered
2. specific	final	detailed	difficult
3. stormy	temperate	mild	desert
4. ambition	command	battle	siege
5. flexible	brittle	pliable	variable
6. chaos	society	history	civilization
7. devastate	destroy	derive	devote

Skills Review: Selections 8–14
Core Skills Reading Comprehension, Grade 7

Your art teacher has assigned you a painting to research and study at the local art museum. It is by the French Impressionist painter Claude Monet and was painted in 1880. Answer the questions below about how to proceed in your research.

1. Circle the letters of the three *most* relevant references.

   a. *Great Masterpieces of France in the 1800s*

   b. *European Art and Artists*

   c. a magazine article about collages

   d. *Art in America*

   e. *The Best of French Artists: 1600–1800*

   f. *Children of Famous Painters*

   g. *A Guide to European Painters*

2. Circle the letters of the four experts that will be *most* helpful to you.

   a. your art teacher

   b. a friend who is taking painting lessons

   c. the director of the city art museum

   d. the man who runs the local art supply shop

   e. the head librarian in the art library

   f. a neighbor who collects art

   g. a man in the paint section at the local hardware store

3. Look at these authors and the books they have written. Circle the letters of the three authors who will *most likely* provide you with relevant information.

   a. Emile Dubois, *German Abstract Art in the 1800s*

   b. Mary Goodfellow, the editor of the *Art Digest*

   c. Jeff Romero, *A Look at the Impressionists*

   d. Tanisha Wright, *Start Painting!*

   e. Mai Wong, *From Albers to Zola: A Look at Great Artists and Their Patrons*

4. Circle the letters of the three *most* useful key words you should type into an Internet search engine.

   a. Expressionism

   b. French+artists

   c. Impressionism

   d. Monet

   e. ancient+art

Name _____ Date _____

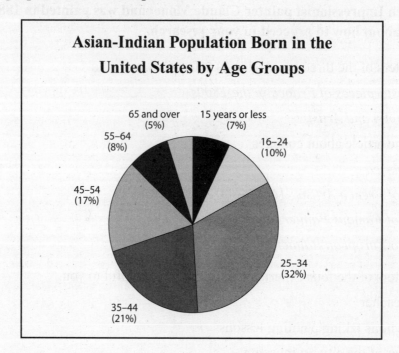

Asian-Indian Population Born in the United States by Age Groups

65 and over (5%)
15 years or less (7%)
16–24 (10%)
55–64 (8%)
45–54 (17%)
25–34 (32%)
35–44 (21%)

1. What percentage of the Asian-Indian people born in the United States are 65 and over?

   a. 10 percent

   b. 17 percent

   c. 5 percent

   d. 8 percent

2. What percentage of the Asian-Indian people born in the United States are ages 16 to 24?

   a. 17 percent

   b. 10 percent

   c. 28 percent

   d. 8 percent

3. Based on the circle graph, which statement below is true?

   a. Most Asian-Indian people born in the United States are teenagers.

   b. Most Asian-Indian people born in the United States are over the age of 65.

   c. Most Asian-Indian people born in the United States are female.

   d. Most Asian-Indian people born in the United States are under the age of 54.

4. What is the largest Asian-Indian age group in the United States?

   a. 35–44   c. 55–64

   b. 45–54   d. 25–34

Answer Key

Selection 1
pages 1–7

A 1. c   3. a
     2. d   4. b

B 1. The effect of the repeated *bl-* sounds is comical and makes Jared sound like someone who should not be taken seriously.
     2. Danny's attitude toward the challenge of going down the rapids is that, despite his small size, he is determined to do it. At first the narrator wants to give up on going in deep water. Later, with his sister's help, he is determined to learn to swim and practices enough to achieve his goal.

C 1. Yes. The mood is a pleasant one when the narrator says that the "contrast between the hot afternoon sun and the cool water was delicious." But when he is faced by the deep water in the swimming hole—dark and seemingly bottomless—the mood is threatening.
     2. Yes. The reader learns important things about the main character, the narrator, because the setting is a river and riverbank where a family reunion is being held. Until the narrator overcomes his fear of deep water and learns to swim, he feels at ease only when the water is shallow.
     3. Yes. The main character, the narrator, is afraid of deep water because he cannot swim. He has to struggle against the river.
     4. Yes. When the narrator is sitting with the adults, parts of the setting are that the heat is increasing and his cousins' happy voices are coming from the direction of the river. This setting helps him to change his mind and try to go in the river.

     Answers will vary as to which function of the setting is most important.

D 1. obnoxious   10. dunking
     2. blithering   11. enthusiastic
     3. panicked   12. basked
     4. reunion   13. embarrassment
     5. balked   14. squishing
     6. shriveled   15. agony
     7. imitating   16. memorable
     8. initiation   17. rapids
     9. genuinely   18. animated

E 1. Jared was a hurtful teaser.
     2. Jared would choose one of the young kids to pick on.
     3. Jared thought the narrator's swimming style was hilarious.

     4. Principal Jones was asking for help with the physical labor.
     5. Karim didn't fit in at school.
     6. The hikers slept deeply and didn't move.

Selection 2
pages 8–18

A 1. b   4. a
     2. d   5. c
     3. a

B 1. Cole's dad is happy because he has just bought the farm and is looking forward to showing it to Cole the next day. He is unaware of Cole's concern about his arriving late. Cole has just gotten over being worried about his dad and is irritated that his dad looks happy.
     2. The mood is peaceful. The phrases "graceful trees" and "rays sparkled on the water," as well as the images of trees bowing over a narrow creek and the creek babbling like child, help to create this mood.
     3. It shows that Cole and his dad are really close; it shows that Cole's dad wants to create a reason to spend time with his son.

C 2. trees—live oaks, cottonwoods
     3. years—40
     4. former owner—agent
     5. box—pocketknife
     6. overnight bag—Cole stays at his dad's on weekends. This is a clue that his parents are separated or divorced.

D 1. a. Detail   4. a. Detail
       b. Main Idea   b. Main Idea
       c. Detail   c. Detail
     2. a. Detail   5. a. Detail
       b. Detail   b. Main Idea
       c. Detail   c. Detail
       d. Main Idea   d. Detail
     3. a. Main Idea
       b. Detail
       c. Detail
       d. Detail

E 1. Cole might want to use the library to find out about the Medal of Honor; he might want to use the Internet to look up a Medal of Honor site; he may want to write to a branch of the military.
     2.–4. Cole should probably look through the house first to find out other information; he might visit the local courthouse or county website; he might want to interview older neighbors to see if they

remember Horace; Cole could use the Internet to find out what branch of the service Horace Mickel was in and more about why his medal was awarded to him.

F Answers will vary. Selection chart should include some of the research steps given in Activity E and the prediction about who Horace Mickel is. The chart should provide a beginning, a middle, and an end.

G 1855, 1861, 1863, 1864, 1865, 1866, 1919
  1855 Mary Walker becomes a doctor.
  1861 Cares for wounded from the Battle of Bull Run.
  1863 Serves close to battlefield.
  1864 Captured by Confederates, then released.
  1865 Awarded Medal of Honor.
  1866 Speaks out for women's right to vote.
  1919 Dies. Nineteenth Amendment is passed.

Selection 3
pages 19–25

A 1. c   5. c
  2. d   6. b
  3. a   7. d
  4. b

B 1. Chris thinks in the same cheerful, optimistic way at the end as he does at the beginning. It is only the narrator who changes her way of thinking. At the beginning, she believes there will be nothing exciting about middle school for Chris; by the end, however, she understands that, because of how he is, he might find it exciting.
  2. A middle-school girl tries to convince her brother that having a locker in middle school will not be as exciting as he thinks. She explains the four unwritten laws that make having a locker an unpleasant situation. Because of his cheerful nature, she fails to convince him.

C 1. Answers will vary.
  2. Answers will vary.

D 1. cheerful—depressed
  2. reject—accept
  3. serious—humorous
  4. scatter—gather
  5. tightening—stretching
  6. amazing—ordinary
  7. protect—attack
  8. unashamed—embarrassed
  9. departed—arrived
  10. rested—struggled

E 1. bashful   6. industrious
  2. attach   7. reality
  3. siblings   8. balance
  4. persist   9. consequences
  5. highlight

F 1. 4 p.m.
  2. Bus students
  3. a pass from the principal, a note from parents or guardians, a list of math questions
  4. a sign-up sheet
  5. a list of math questions and problems
  6. 8 a.m.
  7. the Sierra Room in the library
  8. so they have a good, quiet atmosphere for studying and reading.

Selection 4: Paired
pages 26–29

A 1. b   4. c
  2. a   5. a
  3. c   6. b

B 1. The author probably wants the reader to get a sense of what the Wright brothers were facing when trying to reach their goal; the author wants the reader to get "inside the heads" of the Wright brothers.
  2. Their father's gift of a flying toy "ignited their passion" in "anything that could fly." Lilienthal's unsuccessful experiment with a glider made the brothers want to improve on and go beyond his work.

C 1. O   7. O
  2. F   8. F
  3. O   9. F
  4. F   10. O
  5. O   11. F
  6. F

Selection 5: Paired
pages 30–34

A 1. a   4. d
  2. c   5. a
  3. c   6. c

B The author says that the Wright brothers' approach was better due to their insistence on testing and experimenting in order to have reliable data.

C 1. establish   5. discouraging
  2. unreliable   6. aloft
  3. background   7. manufacturer
  4. fulfillment

116

D 1. no   4. no
   2. yes; 6, 7, 8   5. yes; 8
   3. no   6. yes; 8, 11

E 1. Both authors seem to admire the Wright brothers' determination, but the author of "Soaring High" is much more direct in her admiration. She says that they "gave the world the freedom to soar above the clouds" and they changed the world forever because of their experiments and inventions. The only evidence of the admiration on the part of the "The Wright Brothers" author is her detail that, rather than be discouraged by Lilienthal's doomed experiment with the glider, they started reading everything they could about flying. Also, their determination can be inferred through the details of the work they carried out for more than three years.

   2. The author of "The Wright Brothers" does not address later effects at all. The author of "Soaring High" mentions that the Wright brothers changed the world forever because of their experiments and inventions. Not only did they invent the first flying machine, but they also devised experimental methods that are still being used today.

F 1. SH   5. WB
   2. WB   6. WB
   3. SH   7. SH
   4. SH

Selection 6
pages 35–43

A 1. c   4. c
   2. d   5. a
   3. a

B 1. The brothers use Wes's win as an excuse to eat beignets. This supports the author's idea that food is one of the three things they love most.
   2. The author names the smells of red pepper and other spices; the sound of catfish sizzling on grills; and sights such as pink shrimp floating in soup pots, shelves lined with sweet-potato pies, and crab cakes bigger than dessert plates.
   3. Answers will vary.

C 1. North America
   2. United States
   3. Louisiana
   4. swampy, hot and humid, with wildlife like muskrats and alligators
   5. Cajun land, jambalaya country

D 1. true   7. true
   2. false   8. true
   3. true   9. true
   4. false   10. true
   5. false   11. true
   6. false   12. false

E 1. M   6. M
   2. M   7. S
   3. S   8. S
   4. M   9. M
   5. S   10. S

F Answers may vary depending on dictionary used.
   2. Carib or Arawak Indian—a dugout canoe
   3. French—a fried square doughnut
   4. American French—a spicy stew
   5. Taino or Carib Indian—a fire pit with wood for cooking
   6. Acadian French and American Indian—a creek
   7. Latin—a time of celebration
   8. African—a green vegetable

Selection 7
pages 44–50

A 1. c   4. d
   2. d   5. a
   3. a   6. b

B 1, 5, 3, 7, 2, 9, 4, 6, 8 or 1, 7, 3, 6, 2, 9, 4, 5, 8

C 1. blackened—darkened
   2. potential—possible
   3. exert—apply
   4. show—demonstrate
   5. outside—exterior
   6. emerge—appear
   7. continue—sustain
   8. dispute—oppose
   9. industrious—hardworking
   10. rebellion—protest
   11. theory—idea

D 1. apparatus   6. catalog
   2. flora   7. kinetic energy
   3. specimen   8. dowel
   4. species   9. cargo
   5. principle   10. demonstrate

E 1. h   6. f
   2. e   7. i
   3. a   8. c
   4. g   9. d
   5. b

Skills Review: Selections 1–7
pages 51–55

A Underline:
Paragraph 1: However, chameleons live in many different habitats all over the continent of Africa and on the island country of Madagascar just off the coast of Africa.
Paragraph 2: The rain forest is ideal for chameleons.
Paragraph 3: Chameleons are reptiles, or cold-blooded crawling animals.
Paragraph 4: Chameleons are also lizards, but they differ from other lizards in a few ways.
Paragraph 5: Chameleons have bulging, heavy-lidded eyes that are unique.
Paragraph 6: This special color-changing feature makes chameleons of interest to scientists.

1. b   **3.** a
2. d   **4.** e

B **1.** ferocious—tame   **5.** enlist—resign
2. resist—join   **6.** release—seize
3. camouflaged—exposed   **7.** actual—fantasy
4. regulated—uncontrolled

C Underline opinions:
Paragraph 1: It is sad that such an advanced culture is no more.
Paragraph 2: Perhaps the Maya were looking for some peace after all their troubles.
Paragraph 3: Gold is difficult for everyone to resist since it is so beautiful.
Summary:
      The Mayan civilization began to weaken around AD 900. They began to leave their cities and customs. To escape enemies, they moved their capital to a walled city called Mayapan. When the Spanish came for gold, they began to slowly conquer the Maya. By 1697 all Maya were under the Spanish. When Mexico won its independence in 1821, the Maya tried unsuccessfully to reclaim their lands.

D Paragraphs will vary.

E **1.** b   **3.** a
2. a   **4.** c

Selection 8
pages 56–64

A **1.** d   **5.** b
2. d   **6.** d
3. b   **7.** a
4. c

B After introducing the two sports, the author describes the general features of in-line skates and ice skates that are similar, then points out the differences between the same feature on each type of skate.

C In-line Skates and Ice Skates
I.
   A.
      2. Both let a skater skate well all the time.
      3. Both can be used in more than one sport.
   B.
      1. Both have boots that help support the ankles.
II.
   A.
      2. In-line skates have a plastic boot. Ice skates have a leather boot.
      3. In-line skates have a removable, washable liner. Ice skates do not have a liner.
   B.
      1. In-line skates have wheels.
      2. Ice skates have blades.
   C.
      1. In-line skates have brakes.
      2. Ice skates do not have brakes. Ice skaters use their legs and feet to stop.

D **1.** b   **3.** b
2. d   **4.** d
5. Ice skating is an older sport and has skaters of all ages; people in colder U.S. climates learn to ice skate on local ponds and lakes when they are young.

E **1.** ice skating
2. in-line skating
3. The comparisons all indicate that the weather is cold, winter weather.
4. She says her wheels "whine. . . singing and clicking" like the noises a dolphin makes.
5. Heat waves bouncing off shiny objects makes the atmosphere look like it shimmers and shifts.

F **1.** fabric   **6.** mileage
2. splintering   **7.** perspiration
3. limber   **8.** embarrassment
4. sports   **9.** paper
5. skate wheels

G **1.** The measurement was approximate, but not exact.
2. Because she is ambitious, she wants to make the Honor's List.
3. The green leaves fell in the pond water and began to deteriorate.
4. He had missed out on the fundamentals of algebra and was behind in the class.
5. She is a dancer and is very limber.

118

H 1. tireless   5. strenuous
    2. spirited   6. unfailing
    3. lively   7. strong
    4. energetic   8. unweary

Selection 9
pages 65–73

A 1. c   3. a   5. b
    2. d   4. **d**

B 1. In ancient times, people had fewer resources available to do things such as cure diseases, preserve and season food, and dye cloth. When people realized that some spices accomplished these things, they were willing to spend money to obtain them.
    2. The author seems to find their history fascinating, and he wants the reader to appreciate their history and not simply take salt and spices for granted.

C Salt and Spices
I.
  B. Pepper
    1. Grows on shrubs as a berry
  C.
    1. From the female parts of purple saffron crocus flower
    2. One of most expensive spices in world
    3. Yellow-orange powder
    4. Slender red threads
II.
  A.
    1. Seasoning
    2. Preserving food
    3. Medicine
    4. Preserving bodies
    5. Pay and coins
  B.
    1. Gifts for royalty
    2. Medicine for heart and kidneys
  C. Saffron
    1. Seasoning
    2. Medicine
    3. Honoring guests
    4. Dyeing cloth
    5. Making perfumes
    6. Dyeing hair
    7. Sign of wealth and power
III.
  C. Portugese explorer challenged Arab control in 1498
  D. British traders
    1. Queen Elizabeth I involved in India in 1600s
    2. British East India Company
    3. Controlled spice trade by 18th century

IV.
  A. British tax on salt in India
  B. Mohandas Gandhi's march to sea in protest

D 1. passive   6. preserve
    2. sovereign   7. alliance
    3. nonviolent   8. blockade
    4. evaporates   9. resistance
    5. season

E Across   Down
    1. sal dare   2. dryers
    3. pepper   5. blockades
    4. shrub   7. unless
    6. opens   9. trial
    8. skate
  10. Egypt
  11. daisies
  12. salt

F Time Line
  3,000 BC   Chinese write about salt as medicine.
  27 BC   People in Egypt and Rome use saffron as a cloth dye.
  AD 408   Alaric I demands pepper to stop attack.
  AD 600s   Arab traders conquer India.
  1498   Vasco da Gama challenges Arabs in India.
  mid-1500s   Ladies in court of Henry VIII use saffron as a hair dye.
  1600s   Queen Elizabeth I sends traders to India.
  1700s (18th c.) British secure spice trade in India.
  1930   Gandhi walks to sea to protest unfair British laws.

Selection 10
pages 74–83

A 1. c   4. d
    2. d   5. a
    3. b   6. b

B 1. Her bats were strong enough to have pups despite their problems.
    2. observant: She had observed her bats so carefully that she knew which ones made certain sounds.
    persistent: For two weeks, she did not give up trying to identify which bat had been "singing."

C Summaries may vary. Example:
    Barbara French takes care of bats that have been injured and have to live in captivity. When French's bats began acting strangely, she was anxious about these changes and asked Amanda Lollar, an expert in the care of captive Mexican free-tailed bats, what

119

was happening. French learned that the singing and fighting were mating behaviors. These behaviors stopped once the female bats started having pups. Both French and scientists who study bats learned a lot about the mating behaviors of Mexican free-tailed bats from this experience.

D Answers may vary.
Paragraph 1: SD, SR, M, SD, SD, SD, SD, SR, SR
Paragraph 2: M, SD, SD, SD, SD, SD
Paragraph 3: M, SD, SD, SD
Paragraph 4: SD, M, SD
Paragraph 5: SR, M, SD, SD, SD, SD, SR
Paragraph 6: SD, M, SD
Paragraph 7: SD, M, SD, SD, SD, SD
Paragraph 8: M, SD, SD, SD, SD, SD, SD, SD, SD
Paragraph 9: SD, SD, SR, M, SD

E
1. pollinators
2. roosting
3. compete
4. echolocation
5. membrane
6. nocturnal
7. fertilizer
8. excursion
9. squabble
10. environment/territory

Four Positive Things That Bats Do
(Answers will vary.)

Bats are <u>insectivores</u> and keep the insect population in check.
Bats are <u>pollinators</u> and increase crop production.
Undigested seeds in bat <u>guano</u> grow new plants, like fruit trees.
Bat <u>guano</u> makes excellent <u>fertilizer</u>.

F
1. Hypothesis: The temperature has risen above freezing, causing melting. Proof: Put a temperature gauge, or thermometer, outside to see if the temperature has risen above 32 degrees F.
2. Hypothesis: An earthquake is happening. Proof: After the shaking stops, check the news stations for reports of a quake.
3. Hypothesis: My frog is not as good a jumper as my friend's frog. Proof: Repeat the experiment by holding a series of jumping tests. If my frog continues to be slow, I know my hypothesis is correct.

G Likenesses: Both have ears that are set on the head; both can hear between 2 decibels and 20 decibels; both have like structures—eardrum, eustachian tube, cochlea.

Differences: Ear of bat sits up high on head like an antenna; human ear fits close and low on head; bat ear receives sound at higher levels, from 20 to 40 decibels; human ear has shorter eustachian tube.

Selection 11: Paired
pages 84–88

A
1. peril
2. oppression
3. scanty
4. sublime
5. perpetual
6. sentiment
7. deplorable
8. consecrated
9. clad
10. mingle

B
2. goods available to be distributed
3. loot taken after a battle
4. a class of people with the same characteristics
5. a detailed account or narration
6. the principal nature of something

C
1. a
2. a
3. c
4. d

D
1. Only 17,000 men in Washington's army could have effectively fought a battle; he had to watch his soldiers suffer greatly.
2. Marshall wrote that the conditions described were worse than at any other period of the war.
3. Details are given about how they did not have enough food, blankets or straw, clothing or shoes; that their feet bled; that their huts were "comfortless."
4. Lossing said that despite the harsh weather conditions, the soldiers were still patriotic and willing to fight for their country.

Selection 12: Paired
pages 89–94

A
1. c
2. a
3. b
4. d
5. d
6. a

B
1. The word means "to choke." The use of the word creates an image of the British choking—slowly killing—the rights of free Americans. In this image, rights are equivalent to the air necessary to live.
2. The author lets the reader know that Sarah is willing to ignore her fatigue each time she remembers the hardship that her brother and other soldiers are experiencing.
3. The tears Sarah sheds in the third paragraph are brought on purely by a deep sadness for her brother's suffering. By contrast, the tears she sheds at the end are motivated by a joy that she has probably reduced her brother's and the other soldiers' suffering somewhat, as well as by sadness that they have to be in such a desperate situation.

120

Answer Key

C 1. "I can't be there besides James. But there must be *something* I can do to contribute toward the cause he's willing to die for."

2. Answers will vary.

D 1. "The Letter"

2. The excerpt says that the soldiers "sank into the grave almost unnoticed." Yet in "The Letter" the soldiers were brought supplies and letters of appreciation.

3. The descriptions are very similar. In both selections, the reader learns that the soldiers were exposed to cold and lacked food, shoes, clothes, and blankets.

4. The purposes are similar. The author most likely wrote *Washington at Valley Forge* to describe the suffering and loyalty of Washington's troops during their encampment at Valley Forge. The author of "The Letter" had this same purpose, but he also wanted to tell a story of a sister who does what she can to contribute to the cause of the Revolution.

5. The tone of "The Letter" is sympathetic and uplifting: The author feels for Sarah and her family because James is away at war, yet in the end they are able to help him and his fellow soldiers. The tone of the excerpt is also sympathetic, as the author describes the hardship endured by the troops. Yet it is also one of admiration: The author admires the soldiers' continued loyalty to Washington despite the hardships they had to endure.

6. Answers will vary.

E 1. AA BB CC DD; every two lines end with a rhyming word

2. He made a contraction of over: o'er.

3. Answers will vary. Example: The rhyme scheme and the regular rhythm of the syllables create a sense of the monotony of the soldiers' lives. This gives emphasis to the idea that the "hunger, toil, and pain" were not experienced just once, or just off and on, but repeatedly and all the time.

Selection 13
pages 95–100

A 1. b   4. a
2. d   5. c
3. a

B 1. Answers will vary. Example: She tries to work on any guilt Carlos might feel about not coming home.

2. Several times Daniella mentions that she misses Carlos and that she really wants him to come home for Thanksgiving. This shows that she loves him. She likes being with him, as shown by her description of their camping trip. She also admires him, as shown by her mentioning that he led his football team to the district playoffs.

C 1. rules showing the polite way to behave on the Internet

2. You might get banned from ever posting anything again on a website.

3. Typing in capital letters means you are shouting.

4. include personal attacks, hurtful language, or bad words

5. Some web visitors might not understand what you are saying.

D 1. b   5. a
2. a   6. b
3. b   7. a
4. a   8. b

Selection 14
pages 101–108

A 1. d   3. a   5. c
2. d   4. b   6. d

B 1. The Mexicans were outnumbered and were not as well equipped as the French troops.

2. The information in these paragraphs gives the reader background on why the French troops were in Mexico and helps the reader understand why Mexicans were determined to fight to get the French out of their country.

3. Because Mexico could not pay back the money it owed other countries, troops from those countries arrived in Mexico to collect it. The French stayed, hoping to rule over Mexico, and it was French troops that were defeated in the Battle of Puebla.

4. The author believes that all Americans should observe and celebrate Cinco de Mayo. His reason is that the Mexicans' victory at the Battle of Puebla was indirectly a factor in the Confederates' defeat, which led to the United States remaining one country.

C 1. valor   6. significant
2. historic   7. commanded
3. temporary   8. superior
4. expulse   9. accumulated
5. financial

D **1.** Order of Experts
    a. the head of the Hispanic Studies department at the local college
    b. the director of the Mexican culture section of the local art museum
    c. your history teacher at school
    d. the head librarian at the local city library
  2. Questions will vary.

E Answers will vary. Any topic relating to Cinco de Mayo is acceptable.

F **1.** a, d, e, f, g
  2. b, c, e, g
  3. b, d, e

Skills Review: Selections 8–14
pages 109–114

A **Underline:**
Paragraph 1: If your answer to any of these important questions is yes, then you should take a speech class.
Paragraph 2: There are so many good reasons to take a speech class that it's hard to know where to begin. Taking a speech class makes you confident.
Paragraph 3: In a speech class, you'll learn to think before you speak.
Paragraph 4: Thinking before speaking can make you confident, and this is what you'll practice in a speech class.
Paragraph 5: Speech class will teach you how to prepare and rehearse a speech.
Paragraph 6: Speech class will help you learn about adding zip and spice by having you ask yourself questions.
Paragraph 7: Learning about what not to talk about is just as important as learning what you *should* talk about.
Paragraph 8: Speech class teaches that relating a few main ideas well will capture your audience's attention.
Paragraph 9: And after you finish speech class, no one will ever see your knees shaking again.
  1. d
  2. c

B Answers will vary.

C **1.** bury
  2. hand
  3. joke
  4. observe

D **1.** b
  2. a
  3. d
  4. c
  5. d

E **1.** irrigated—watered
  2. specific—detailed
  3. temperate—mild
  4. battle—siege
  5. flexible—pliable
  6. society—civilization
  7. devastate—destroy

F **1.** a, b, g
  2. a, c, e, f
  3. b, c, e
  4. b, c, d

G **1.** c
  2. b
  3. d
  4. d